Popular Glass
of the
19th & 20th Centuries

A Collector's Guide

MILLER'S

Popular Glass
of the
19th & 20th Centuries

A Collector's Guide

Raymond Notley

MILLER'S POPULAR GLASS: A COLLECTOR'S GUIDE
by Raymond Notley

First published in Great Britain in 2000 by Miller's, a division of
Mitchell Beazley, imprints of Octopus Publishing Group Ltd,
2–4 Heron Quays, London E14 4JP

First published in the USA in 2000
Copyright © Octopus Publishing Group Ltd 2000
Miller's is a registered trademark of Octopus Publishing Group Ltd
This edition distributed in the USA by Antique Collectors' Club Ltd.,
Market Street Industrial Park, Wappingers' Falls, New York, NY 12590, USA

Commissioning Editor **Liz Stubbs**
Executive Art Editor **Vivienne Brar**
Editors **Selina Mumford & Samantha Ward-Dutton**
Designer **Louise Griffiths**
Indexer **Sue Farr**
Proofreader **Laura Hicks**
Illustrator **Amanda Patton**
Production **Nancy Roberts**
Specially commissioned photography by **AJ Photographs**
Jacket photograph by **Steve Tanner**

The publishers will be grateful for any information that will assist them in
keeping future editions up to date. Although all reasonable care has been
taken in the preparation of this book, neither the publishers nor the
compilers can accept any liability for any consequence arising from the use
thereof, or the information contained therein.

ISBN 1 84000 286 7
A CIP catalogue record for this book is available from the British Library
Set in Bembo, Frutiger, and Shannon
Colour reproduction by HK Scanner Arts INT'L Ltd.
Produced by Toppan Printing Co., (HK) Ltd.
Printed and bound in China
Half-title page: Blue pressed-glass jardinière, $94–320;
contents page: BAROLAC three-branch candlestick in opalescent
glass, $640, pair $1,600

contents

Introduction

The British Industrial Revolution of the late 18thC rose on the back of the production of iron. Machinery, accurately made of fine metals, and efficiently powered by steam, made inroads into all aspects of consumer production, from agriculture to the mass manufacture of household goods.

The basic craft of glass, made by a noble band of workers, incumbents of an ancient tradition, had remained virtually unchanged, except by those variations dictated by the sophistications of fashion, since the glories of Imperial Rome.

Glass was heavily taxed by weight in the British Isles, with the exception of Ireland, from 1745 to 1845. It languished in Britain as a somewhat old-fashioned and – because of its cost, exaggerated by the heaviness of the favored lead glass – rather élitist material. The inevitable mechanization, leading to the democratization of glass production, occurred in the rapidly industrializing U.S.A. during the first quarter of the 19thC. Ironically enough, the prohibitive British glass tax was one of the many taxes imposed to raise money for the wars with America!

The popularization of glass occurred for three reasons. Firstly, the basic ingredients of glass, sand and soda, were cheap. Secondly, machinery obviated the expense involved in the individual production of glass items, as well as ensuring a standardization of shape and form. Thirdly, its plastic nature was perfect for machine replication. Output per worker increased dramatically as molded goods were produced in rapid sequence by machine operatives rather than laboriously by skilled artisans. The skills of glassmaking passed from the craftsman glassblower to the manufacturers of presses, and the chippers of hinged molds, which were used in machines.

For the first time, items made of glass became objects of everyday domestic use, rather than items associated with the luxurious consumption of food and drink. There had been cheap glass, of course, but it was crude and almost brutally functional. The new machine glass was attractive and readily available.

The early history of the development of machinery in the U.S.A. has been reconstructed evidentially, as the documentary records of all the unnumbered U.S. patents of the important early 19thC period, dating back to 1791, were destroyed in a fire at the U.S. Patent Office in December 1836.

Simple presses, producing simple goods, were improved toward the mid-century, and both the mechanics and the products became more sophisticated, and even more attractive to the consumer.

In the 1860s, gas was in use for melting glass in Europe, and the 1870s saw the increasing use of free natural gas in the U.S. glass industry. British plants remained faithful to coal, coke, and oil, with some use of gas. Pressing techniques were perfected in the 1880s, when the complexity and ingenuity of the molds, and the sophisticated facility of the machinery, became the slaves of rapid, and eclectic, changes in fashionable taste. In the 1880s, glass was also increasingly melted in continuously flowing tanks, rather than in the traditional single ceramic pot.

Popular glass was a 19thC phenomenon that gave rise to a huge industry which was already in eclipse by 1900. Up to 1900, people had worked the machines, pulling levers, dropping glass into molds, and often adjusting the soft forms as they were molded into fancy variations before they cooled. Gradually the machine could do everything, and this was signalled in the late 19thC by the fully automatic production of bottles, jars, and similar packaging goods for the food and drink industry.

An adjunct to pressing was the technique of blow-molding, in hinged molds, of hollow vessels with narrow necks, which were impossible to press-mold. This was an ancient technique, but it became increasingly precise with the use of complex 19thC iron molds.

Some factories still produce glassware using hand-operated pressing machinery, but they survive by manufacturing from either old molds, or new molds in nostalgic forms.

On this page can be seen some neatly pressed items of tableware from an extensive suite of matching items which was made at Gateshead, Tyne and Wear, in the 1880s, and marked by Davidson's. The design is based on expensive, sparkling, hand-made, hand-cut and polished, lead glass. This ability of mold-makers to mimic expensive hand techniques was the basis of the popularity of pressed, clear, flint glass. It is interesting to compare this with the imposing covered urn on the opposite page, which is in the Neo-classical style. This has crisp

molding of well-ordered panels, strong horizontal banding, and imitation strawberry diamond and hobnail "cutting." The urn dates from the period 1925–30, when there was a great revival of late 18C taste; this had started between 1900 and 1914, and included reproductions of the furniture designs of Sheraton and Chippendale. Some glassware of the 1920s and 1930s was named after these designers. The red glass contains selenium and copper, and was a technical innovation of the mid 1920s. Previously, red glass had needed gold salts, and had been difficult to press successfully with any retention of fine detail.

This urn was sold in pairs, and is known in dark green as well as clear glass. Where it was made is uncertain, as it is unmarked, but from its characteristics, and from documented items in similar style and colors, it is probably Czech or German. The price for the complete water set shown above would be around $160, with one covered urn costing the same.

Prices
Prices for antiques vary, depending particularly on the condition of the item, but also according to geographical location, and market trends. The price ranges given throughout the book should be seen as a general indicator to value only.

Early pressed glass

Pressed glass from the 1820s to the 1850s is characterized by a series of technical advancements, which are about refinement of form, the overcoming of mechanical problems, the increasing complexity of hinged molds, and a growing fluency and confidence of production. The glass industries in Belgium, France, and Bohemia expanded during the 1830s, and were soon producing crisply molded articles in a variety of colored opaque and tinted clear glass. The fashionable revivals of the early 19thC, such as Gothic, Rococo, and the eclectic combinations beloved in the 1840s, all appear on pressed glass of this period.

▼ Cup plates
These two cup plates from the 1840s, of the same design, with variant base patterns, are probably from Belgium, but were of U.S. inspiration. Many similar U.S. examples exist; those with patriotic symbols, such as the eagle, are now rare and expensive. The molds used for the two plates below probably had loose, and interchangeable, base plates. This technical advance enabled apparent novelty and variation to be produced from one mold.

Clear glass salt dish by the Boston & Sandwich Glass Company, 1830–40, **$80** in clear, rising to **$320** in emerald green

▲ Clear glass salt dish
Produced by the Boston & Sandwich Glass Company, this eclectic pattern, with its ornate feet and baskets of flowers, framed by curvaceous scrolls and stylized blooms, is also known in opaque white, grayish-blue and emerald-green glass. Similar dishes, in the form of paddle steamers, are worth 50% more.

Cup plates, 1840s, **$32** in clear, and **$48** in blue

Handles

Most early handles were added by hand, but this process became obsolete as technically advanced molds made it possible to incorporate a normally proportioned handle into the molding process. Some early items do have huge molded handles that are disproportionately large. Obviously, the handlers were soon out of work.

Pressed-glass plates, 1835–40, **$64** each, or **$48** for smaller versions

▲ Pressed-glass plates

The early English pressed-glass plate on the right shows a portrait of the young Queen Victoria, surrounded by shamrocks, thistles and roses. These representations of Ireland, England, and Scotland are common on 19thC glass. Few references to Wales occur. Some smaller examples exist, and some have a small "W," thought to be the mark of the mold-cutter. The floral bouquet plate, borrowed from contemporary French designs, is finely stippled, and uses Neo-classical and Rococo ideas as a border. Smaller cup-plate versions of this design are known. These are signed with the initials "WR," believed to be those of a Birmingham die-cutter, rather than a factory indicator.

▼ Creamer

This early English creamer, or small milk jug, of around 1845 is thickly molded from a clear and sparkling glass. It is derived from Neo-classical cut-glass forms, and is emphatically horizontal in its layered geometry. The handle has been applied by hand, with the twist of glass first being applied to the rim, looped up, and then down, to be attached, with a flourish, just above the base. The handle has a limpid fluidity when compared with the angularity of the jug itself.

Clear milk jug, or creamer, with applied handle, c.1845, **$64**

Clear glass stemmed sugar bowl, 1845, **$40**

▲ Sugar bowl

Made around 1845, this English, stemmed sugar bowl is of heavy, thick, and chunky construction. The mark of the centre seam of the mold can be seen, running down the centre of the piece. This massive bowl has a fine air of solid grandeur about it, and is made of a clear and sparkling glass. The mold is a fairly simple form – the weight, and luster, of the glass are the centre of attraction.

Plates & serving dishes

Glass was an elegant and hygienic material for domestic use, and was, because of the 19thC increase of pressed-glass production, cheaply available in an increasingly attractive range of functional shapes. Open salts were needed because free-flowing salt was not generally available until around 1900; bread-and-butter plates were required for most meals; square, rectangular, round, and oval dishes of various sizes were made to accommodate canned fish, and assorted meats, straight from the differently shaped cans; and cold salads, hard-boiled eggs, and cheese straws, as well as endless dainties, cluttered up tables for the impromptu meals known as "high tea" and "supper." Pressed-glass wares for functional use proliferate, and are a good choice for a themed collection.

▼ Gothic revival (1830–51)

Much early pressed glass bears traces of the powerful Gothic revival of the period 1830–1851. In France, which was rapidly industrializing during this period, many finely cut molds were made for many companies, including Baccarat and St Louis. This French open salt stands on three paw feet, which recalls furniture of classical inspiration. The body, however, is angular, and uses arched Gothic architecture for its rhythm, and the rim comes from classical vase sources. French molded glass of this period can often be found in opaque, jet-black, and a sealing-wax red glass.

An oval-shaped salt in clear glass, American, c.1840, **$56–88**

A three-footed French salt in clear glass, late 1830s, **$80–160**

◀ Rococo revival (1830–1840s)

Industrial design of the 19thC often used two or more styles simultaneously, in an attempt to lengthen the consumer attraction of an expensive mold. The fancy U.S. salt of around 1840, shown left, owes its design to the imitation geometric, cut palmette edging, and fluted base, of the 1800–1820 Neo-classical period, in conjunction with the curvaceous, Rococo, scrolled leaves of the growing revival of 18thC taste, which characterizes the 1830s. Pressed glass often imitated fashions in cut glass, as well as making use of general revivals evident in contemporary furniture, and interior design pattern books.

▼ Imitation cut glass (1830–today)

The cutting of iron molds to imitate the vocabulary of hand-cut glass, was one of the methods that did not endear the pressed-glass factories to the older, more traditional manufacturers. Imitation cut glass was a constant offering of pressed-glass production from the 1830s, and remains with us today. Whole suites of tableware were available from the 1860s, and were used both domestically, and by the catering and hotel trades. Oval and round dishes were issued in various sizes that stacked within each other.

▼ Flat plates (1840–today)

There is a vast selection of serving plates made from the 1840s, such as the 1880s hobnail-"cut" plate shown below. These were initially fancy rather than practical; it was not until around 1916, when new, heat-proof, oven glass was introduced, that simple functional plates were introduced. "Pyrex" and "Phoenix" tableware in clear glass were often sold with printed designs, such as the blue Willow Pattern, during the 1930s. Oven-to-tableware was created, and this has been further extended to microwave- and dishwasher-proof glass.

An English, amber, hobnail-"cut" flat serving plate, c.1880, **$48–64**

Practical collecting

The fun of collecting serving dishes lies in the fact that they can actually be used. Recreating food from old recipe books is a growing hobby, and there is a keen demand for appropriate, 19thC, glass serving ware. With care and imagination, quite ordinary and economical food can look spectacularly attractive in dramatic glass tableware. "Harlequin" sets, or mismatching items, are fine, and a selection of stemmed, shallow, and deep bowls will provide the repertoire of dishes needed for an impressive buffet. Of course, with determination, or good luck, you could find a pile of matching items tucked away at a dealer's somewhere. Never use old dishes for hot food, and always wash them by hand as they are not suitable for the harsh, hot monsoons of modern dishwashers.

A molded, imitation hobnail-"cut" serving dish by Davidson, c.1880, **$40–64**

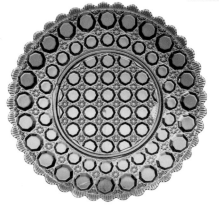

An elaborate serving
dish by Davidson,
c.1890, **$80–96**

A Carnival Glass, handled
comport, in peach opalescent
finish, **$160–240**

▲ "Rustic" serving ware

This attractive dish, with
quartered low divisions, and
a briar-rose design, is a good
example of "rustic" serving
ware. Floral decorations, which
recalled a bucolic past, were
popular with urban dwellers,
who were rapidly losing their
country roots. Partially
emanating from the designs
and ideas of William Morris,
this ruralism reveals itself on
manufactured goods that
depict wild flowers and fruit,
as well as plants, such as ivy,
which are full of symbolism,
and particularly associated
with marriage. Pressed glass
was respectable and attractive
enough to be offered as both
practical and decorative
giftware by the 1890s.

A low three-footed olive or nut
dish, c.1880, **$40–56**

▲ Serving dish for appetizers

This dish has a smooth interior,
but the exterior bears a wild
flower, growing in a natural
manner. The feet and handle
recall the ribbed "shell" type
of applied handle, an 1867
patent of the hand-made glass
factory of Thomas Webb &
Sons. Such feet appear as a
regular feature of pressed glass
from the 1880s. This dainty
item, of ubiquitous function,
is a good example of items
made both in the U.S.A., and
throughout Europe. Zesty
appetizers were fashionable at
this time, as were preserved
olives, and there was a
growing fad for nuts.

▲ Carnival Glass comport

This comport, currently
called the "Starfish" design,
is pressed in opalescent
glass, with milky edging.
The interior was sprayed
with metal salts to give a
golden luster effect. This
combination, known to
modern collectors as peach
opalescent, originally had
odd names such as "Mexican
Aurora." It marks a transition,
from the popular opal finishes
of the late 19thC, to the rising
fashion for iridescence of the
first decade of the 20thC.
This comport was made in
the U.S.A. by the Dugan-
Diamond Glass Co., which
made the bulk of this color
in Carnival Glass.

FACT FILE

Check for cracks

Serving dishes will have been well used, so check carefully for damage, although the level of wear and tear you will accept is up to you as to. Absolute mint–condition pieces should ring alarm bells, as there are modern replicas about, particularly of Depression Glass. Cracked, and severely chipped, items are, however, worthless.

▼ **Depression Glass**

The smooth, very shallow patterns to be found on machine-made tableware of the 1930s reflect the necessity of smooth, continuous, snag-free, mechanical operation. The needs of the machine during the economic crises of the period came first, and the designs, although very attractive, are invariably linear, rather than deeply sculptural. These items were made by the U.S. Macbeth-Evans Co. As with Carnival Glass, there are devotees of Depression Glass, and this design is collected as "American Sweetheart." There are many other shapes with the same design.

A Depression Glass, part serving-plate set, in Monax opalescent glass: set of large plate plus six small, **$64–80**

Nestlé chocolate shell dish, clear glass, c.1935, **$56–80**

▲ **Nestlé shell dish**

This promotional dish, of unknown manufacture, would have been for use in promotional displays, probably for free samples, of the then Swiss-manufactured chocolate products of Nestlé. Many glass items remain from the 1890s, ranging from ashtrays to display jars and comports, with various slogans and manufacturers' names on them. Some were offered for home use from "coupon" campaigns. All are collectible and are still modestly priced.

An attractive dish, Scandinavian, 1930s, **$40–56**

▲ **Scandinavian serving dish**

This good-quality pressing recreates, in a refined manner, similar designs of the second half of the 19thC made in Sweden. The glass is of exceptional quality, and is a sophisticated combination of imitation cutting, in the centre, and panels of formally presented bunches of flowers, in intaglio, on the rear. It is decorative and functional – typical of the inter-war Scandinavian approach.

Celeries & pickles

The 19thC saw colorful ceramics – pots with printed lids – and glass being used as packaging, and these were thought attractive enough to be kept as ornamental novelties. Pickles and preserves were the obvious choice of foods to pack in glass, whereas fish and meat pastes, and quack pomades, were sold in both glass and ceramic containers. Blanched, sweet, and crisp celery became a fashionable table item, especially as a winter tonic, and cheese and celery became part of the Victorian culinary vocabulary. From the 1870s, vast sets of matching tableware invariably included a celery glass, or vase. These remained globally popular, and were still in production until as recently as 1939.

A Manchester-made, cobalt-blue, pickle vase, c.1890, **$96–144**

◀ **Press-molded packaging**
This vivid vase has a rim suitable for a lid of some description, such as waxed paper with a string closure. Other similar designs exist, all made by John Derbyshire, and most have Patent Office Design Registration marks (see p.60), as well as the company mark. These are not rare, but they are becoming scarce as collectors snap them up. There are keen collectors of Manchester-made glass, those who like any British pressed glass, and others who just collect cobalt-blue pressed glass. This does create a sellers' market.

▼ **Urn-shaped celeries**
Stemmed holders are the most common celery glasses. The one shown below is not marked, but it was probably made in France or Belgium. The pedestal bases raised the celery above the level of the table, as well as looking tastefully classical. Vases such as this produce optical effects through the prism-and-lens-like quality of some components of the structure. These vases could also be used simply as decoration, or to hold flowers.

A stemmed, urn-shaped, celery glass, 1880s, **$32–48**

An opaque, marbled, gray, glass celery vase, English, c.1890, **$80–120**

A pressed, red, celery glass, German, c.1932, **$56–72**

Red pressed glass – beware of imitations

Red, and blue, pressed-glass items are collectible in their own right. While blue examples go back to the early 19thC, pressed red glass was technically viable only from the 1920s. Do not buy pressed red glass as "Victorian", even if it looks old-fashioned, and quaint – it isn't.

▼ Sowerby's 1920s tableware

This highly practical celery vase, designed in 1900, inspired an extensive matching range of table glass, introduced by Sowerby around 1924. Some of this "Pineapple" service was iridized with a marigold "Sungold" finish, but not this item, as far as is known. The later molds are probably French. It is an optically lively design, with its angularity softened by the bold central lens, and the ball feet, which offer stability.

▲ Cool marble effects

Commonly called "slag" glass, this type of opaque glass was fashionable from 1880 to 1900. The novelty marble effect was perhaps suggestive of coolness. Glass molded with frosty effects was also popular at this time. Although forms such as this, with optical prisms, and leaf effects, were better intended for clear-glass production, it is typical to find such designs being made in opaque novelty glass, which is not quite in accordance with the original translucent concept. These vases probably spent more time on the chimneypiece than in use on the table.

▲ Red celery glass

The glamour of red glass is compounded by its association with the words "gold" and "ruby." Gold was needed to produce red in glass up to the 1920s, when selenium and copper began to be employed. Most pressed red glass around today is post 1924. The Brockwitz factory in Germany made this item in the 1930s, and it is also found in blue, and marigold, Carnival Glass finishes. There are many other items in this design, which is called "Curved Star." Brockwitz was a major mold-maker, and sold this pattern to other factories.

A square, ball-footed celery vase by Sowerby, 1920s, **$40–48**

Butter, cream, & sugar wares

The elaboration of tea-drinking, and the charade of tea-time, formed a 19thC practise of the English aristocracy, that by 1900 was popular with the middle and working classes. Novelty milk-and-sugar sets were all the rage, and appeared in all the decorative disguises of the period. As well as bread being buttered, it was common to butter toasted tea-cakes, and slices of cake, so fresh butter was served in covered dishes of increasingly elaborate and amusing forms. There were no glass teapots until the 1920s, when heat-proof glass was developed to an esthetically pleasing thinness. Some 19thC glass "teapots" are actually oil-lamp fillers.

▼ Japan and Morris

This attractive, opaque, milk-and-sugar set was pressed in pale ivory yellow by Sowerby at Gateshead. It is marked with PODR for 1880 (see p.60). The pattern recalls "Willow," which was one of William Morris's most popular designs. The handle of the milk jug has a quaint Japanese angularity, which is well in keeping with the Japanese side of the English Esthetic movement, with which Sowerby himself was connected via his "art" juvenilia. Other glass used nursery designs by Walter Crane.

A patriotic milk-and-sugar set in milk glass, c.1880, **$80–120**

A Sowerby, Esthetic milk-and-sugar set in ivory glass, 1880–1890, **$160–280**

▲ Patriotic patterns

This set, of uncertain English manufacture, is pressed from glass made opaque with tin oxide and known as milk glass. The design is of roses for England, shamrock, for Ireland, and thistles for Scotland, and there are many 19thC items so decorated. Wales is rarely depicted. The milk-jug handle and sugar-bowl feet are rusticated, in forms resembling twigs and stumps. Again, these are design notions that appear constantly from 1880–1920.

Milk-and-sugar sets
An ideal choice for new collectors, milk–and–sugar sets exist in generous numbers, and in a huge variety of colors and finishes. They also take up little space, and can be displayed easily. Internationally manufactured, many exist in Carnival Glass iridized form. Some, but not all, will be found to match many other table items. The designs are fantastically diverse, and prices are attractive, but they do rise steadily.

A frosted, Sowerby Rosalin, swan butter-dish, c.1930, **$64–96**

▲ **Swan song**
The Sowerby factory was in financial trouble from well before World War I, and to counteract the depression it recycled many of its old 19thC molds, using the satin-pink and green glass fashionable in the late 1920s and the 1930s. The mold for the swan dish above dates from the 1880s, when the factory made examples with a space between the lower neck and the body. Some Carnival Glass examples from the 1920s, in marigold and purple, with open lower necks, remain. This butter-dish has a filled-in neck, as have some later Carnival Glass versions.

An elaborate, Vallerysthal, covered sugar, French, c.1890, **$240–320**

▲ **The French connection**
The Vallerysthal factory was in the Alsace-Lorraine area annexed by Germany from 1871 to 1919. It is, however, generally regarded as a French factory. It specialized in elaborate, fanciful, often figurative, pressed glassware in a variety of colors, much of which was cold decorated. The design above suggests sweetness, and the item was cataloged as a sucrier (sugar bowl). The color, recalling the *bleu céleste* of Sèvres, is typical of Vallerysthal. The paint has often worn off, giving many such items a sadly distressed look.

▼ **French hens**
Sowerby bought the mold for this chicken butter-dish from France in the mid 1920s. Called "Chic", it was used for Carnival Glass production in iridized marigold and blue, as well as in plain, frosted pink and green. It was in erratic production, and residual stocks were stored until well after World War II. In the 1960s, a release of mint-condition, surplus production of this and various other long-packed-away old and classic items caused much confusion.

A frosted, "Chic" butter-dish by Sowerby, 1930s, **$64–96**

Breakfast & tea wares

Breakfast was ritualized by the English lower social classes during the Edwardian period, when there was a modest increase in general wealth. The upper-class buffet was emulated by elaborate table presentations of preserves in dishes with "silver" spoons, of toast in "letter-rack" holders, of boiled eggs in fancy cups, and condiments in splendid sets of containers. Cookies were increasingly popular, and were usually stored in elaborate barrels, originally made of wood and brass, but increasingly of glass. These were displayed, and the contents were usually reserved for visitors. Glass specimens from the breakfast and tea-time sessions are quite delightful, and can, of course, still be used if you wish to recreate the pleasant formalities of past table manners.

Left to right: A French, opalescent egg cup, c.1908; an English, green egg cup, 1925; both **$24–56**

◀ Egg cups

The opalescent egg cup, far left, is marked Vallerysthal (see p.60), and is from the Edwardian period. The very similar green-glass example bears a British design number of 714837, which dates it from 1925. This obvious plagiarism was quite common. There are many novelty, glass egg cups, and these are space-saving objects to collect. They are not easy to find, but they are rewarding for the patient and assiduous collector. They are still in production, so buy new examples before they disappear!

▼ Toast stands

Glass stands for toast are relatively rare. (Silver and EPNS are much more common.) Such forms needed complex molds, and the item shown below has the added complexity of having open handles molded in. This example is relatively plain, functional, and easy to keep clean. It is a Sowerby design, registered in June 1874, but not trademarked. In turquoise vitro-porcelain, it matched many other household items, such as the plate with stand opposite.

A Sowerby, turquoise, vitro-porcelain toast holder, 1874–1900, **$88–152**

Look for lids

Collecting glass services and unusual items in matching patterns is an absorbing task. "Pearline" is very popular, and is collected in the blue or the "Primrose", just as it was when it was first made. Items with lids are dearer than those without. Spare lids are virtually impossible to find, so buying a butter base or cookie barrel without a lid is not a good idea!

▼ Plates on stands

This wickerwork design is from Sowerby, and consists of a plate resting on a matching "woven" stand. There are both open edging and open work to the base, suggesting a cleverly cut mold of great precision. This plate would have been used to serve anything from iced fancy cakes to fruit. The molds remained in good enough condition to be used for both marigold and purple Carnival Glass production in the late 1920s, when they were also pressed in ruby red. Ruby examples are not Victorian.

A Sowerby, blue, vitro-porcelain cake plate with stand, c.1880
$240–280

A Davidson, blue "Pearline" cake stand, c.1890, **$240–280**

▲ Matching "Pearline"

Following the introduction of the opalescent "Pearline," in 1889, Davidson produced considerable quantities of matching tableware in both blue and "Primrose". Tables and dressers were bedecked with this attractive service, which was inexpensive to buy. Cake stands, such as the one shown above, were ideal for the light sponge, cherry, walnut, and caraway, or seed cakes that were so popular at the time.

▼ Cookie barrels

Bought cookies were a relative luxury, as well as a status symbol. You were judged by your cookie, which was clearly marked with the maker's name, and everyone knew the price! The cookie barrel was a popular serving and storage vessel. Metal and wooden examples were popular, but a matching glass service was not complete without one. This Davidson "Primrose Pearline" example has a fine EPNS rim band and handle. As it was not airtight, crisp cookies soon went soft ...

A Davidson, "Primrose Pearline" cookie barrel, c.1890, **$192–240**

Pitchers & decanters

The availability of cheap, stylish glass brought about a change to the appearance of bourgeois and working-class table-settings of an aspirational nature. This is apparent in the growth from the 1880s of "lemonade" sets, which, of course, could also be used for water or ale. The latter was available at the local public house ("pub"), from the now defunct "jug-and-bottle" servery. Sherry and port both last well in decanters, and molded decanters were popular for special occasions. Residing in the parlor, they were mostly referred to as wine sets – the decanters could indeed have been filled with "claret" at the pub.

A lemonade tumbler and pitcher by Davidson, c.1895; tumbler **$56–72**, pitcher **$120–152**

◀ Lemonade, anyone?

This fine, yellow, opalescent pitcher-and-tumbler set was made by Davidson, at Gateshead, between 1889, when this finish was introduced, and 1910, when its appeal was fading. The yellow finish, called "Primrose Pearline", contained uranium, and the blue version contained cobalt. Both had phosphates added to develop the semi-opaque highlights. Lemonade recipes abounded, and commercial versions quickly followed. Lemonade crystals, mostly sugar, citric acid, and a violent colouring, became popular around 1900 – one brand was sold as "Eiffel Tower" in a now scarce, and very collectable bottle of that shape!

▼ The Roaring 20s

The luxuriousness of the metallic luster finish of Carnival Glass added an allure to the wine sets made, even through Prohibition, in the U.S.A. Pressed-glass sets, imitating cut-glass patterns, by Imperial arrived in the U.K. from 1910, and were available until well into the 1920s. This golden finish complemented the sweet sherries and other wines that were popular at the time. A complete purple set similar to this is quite rare.

A marigold, "Octagon", Carnival Glass wine set by Imperial, U.S.A., c.1920; decanter, stopper, and six glasses, **$280–480**

Collecting sets

Price-determining factors are the production ratio (i.e., one pitcher for six tumblers); the survival ratio (more bases than lids survive from butterdishes, for example); and shapes and colors (some shapes are common, but rare in odd colors). A complete set of something is worth more than the sum of its parts.

A Carnival Glass water set, Finland, 1930s; tumblers **$240–320** each, pitcher **$640–800**

▲ 1930s water set

These tumblers first appeared in the Finnish company Riihimäki's catalogs in the 1930s; they also exist in other, smaller sizes. It is a puzzle that the pitcher, without the tumblers, was also shown in a Buenos Aires glass company's catalog in the early 1930s ... However, metal molds did travel a great deal from 1919 onward, and plagiarism was rife. Scandinavian- and German-made Carnival Glass of the 1930s is now becoming very popular with collectors, as is reflected by rapidly rising prices. The current, superficial explanations of Carnival Glass made outside the U.S.A. in the inter-war period need clarifying.

▼ Plain and simple 1930s chic

This simple blow-molded decanter was made during the 1930s in Czechoslovakia, where much glass was commissioned for sale in France. This simple style is characterized by strong horizontals, which are a general feature of 1930s design. In this case the style also recalls English cut-glass decanters of 1820. Simple, shallow, round trays, and matching, small glasses, complete the set. There are also enamelled sets, usually with floral patterns.

A blow-molded, iridized decanter, Czechoslovakia, 1930s, **$40–64**; with enamelled decoration, **$72–96**

A molded, green, American Depression Glass pitcher, c.1930, **$64–88**

▲ Depression Glass

The U.S. glass industry survived the depression by making glassware produced entirely by automatic means. The glass was cheap, and the designs were shallowly cut into moulds to obviate snags in the production sequence. It was mostly tableware, and was made in vast quantities. The pitcher shown above has a curved-in ice lip to trap ice.

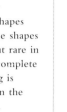

Tumblers & goblets

The tumbler was the first table item to be made in any quantity during the early history of pressed glass. The pattern, if any, was on the exterior of the vessel, and the inside was necessarily smooth. This worked well with a smooth plunger pressing downward to force glass into a simple, two-part, open-and-shut mold. The bases of tumblers were often ground smooth and flat to sit well on a table. Tumbler sizes varied considerably, and they would have been used both in the licenced trade and at home. By the 1850s, and particularly in Britain following the abolition of the Glass Tax in 1845, heavy, chunky goblets were readily available, and became fashionable. They were economically multi-functional, as they were suitable for holding water, wine, and ales. Nowadays many of these items are still eminently suitable for everyday use, as was originally intended.

Two measured, marked, "half pint" tumblers, in marbled "slag" glass, the blue by Davidson, the gray by Sowerby, 1880s, **$112–144** each

▼ "Half-pint" tumblers
It seems somewhat quaint to drink from a glass that is streaked, and opaque, and resembles marble. This glass mixture, opaque with metallic oxides, is called "slag" glass, as it was once assumed that it contained recycled products of the coke and gas industry (see p.34). In poor areas a glass of beer had to last, and it was common to use pewter cups in ale houses. These rare slag glasses show the glass industry attempting to cater for the dignified custom of not revealing how much was left in a vessel.

▶ Tippling and the middle classes
This blue "Pearline" tumbler is typical of glassware made with an opalescent finish. The trick was to put into the glass a phosphate (in this case, actual bone ash), which went opaque as the thickest parts cooled. A blast of compressed air often accelerated and intensified the selective effect. This blue-color effect suggests coolness, and in pre-refrigeration days it would have offered an illusion of freshness. The artistic nature of this tumbler would have alleviated the qualms of the middle classes with regard to alcohol, which was seen as very working-class.

A blue "Pearline" tumbler, also found in "Primrose" yellow, by Davidson, c.1890, **$56–72**

◀ Scarce U.S. Glass Company tumbler, moulded in imitation of the rock-crystal style of the 1880s, c.1910, **$80–96**

▼ Tumblers galore

It is possible to collect a variety of unmarked tumblers, of lively colors and shapes, from a surprising variety of sources, at modest prices. The tumblers can date from the early 1840s up to the present day. While collecting such items is a pleasure, and the results are fascinating, frustration rules with regard to identifying the actual sources and dates of individual items. This is collecting for fun, rather than pedantic documentation. The tumblers shown below are possibly from England, Belgium, and France, but the bistro glass on the right could be from Finland or Russia!

A collection of unmarked tumblers, of unknown origins and ages, **$16–64** depending on color and pattern

▲ The U.S. Glass Company

This superb press-molded tumbler is a high-quality product typical of the co-operative conglomeration of various U.S. factories that operated under the U.S. Glass Company. It established offices and depots in Europe, stretching from London to Constantinople, from the turn of the 20thC, but it had faded away by the late 1920s. The company's ability to produce pressed glass that resembled expensive "Art and Cut Glass" astonished the European popular glass industry, which could not compete.

A goblet in purple iridized glass, by Imperial Glass, U.S.A., c.1914, **$80–112**

▲ Imperial grandeur

This splendid goblet is a good example of the "triple doping" iridizing technique of Imperial Glass of Bellaire, Ohio. The factory's Carnival Glass is, bafflingly, not highly regarded in the U.S.A., but it is highly respected, and avidly collected, elsewhere. This goblet, with grapes on the bowl, is known as "Imperial Grape" by collectors.

Fancy bowls & baskets

By the 1880s, consumers were used to press-molded glass, and, with disposable incomes gradually increasing, manufacturers were able to tempt customers with fancy items that were marginally, rather than totally, functional. These items were attractive in their own right, but they needed to have a token function assigned to them in order to satisfy lingering puritan ethics, which equated useless objects of pure adornment with sin. Working-class and lower-middle-class consumers were the main markets, but these "novelty" items were also desired by higher-class consumers, who added them to household accumulations of knick-knacks; as artistic products of industry they were deemed modern. This was part of the popularization of Estheticism with its worship of "art for art's sake."

▲ Ship ahoy!

Pressed-glass makers and some traditional glass factories launched a flotilla of boat-shaped novelties in the 1880s. Sizes varied from tiny vessels, for spent matches, to larger boats, which were originally parts of sets of matching tableware. Sowerby marketed its confusingly numbered "1874" service in the 1880s. The boat above was originally issued in clear pressed glass to match the service, but was later made available separately in different colors.

A very rare 14" Sowerby boat on original stand, in semi-opaque, sea-green opal glass, c.1885, complete **$1,200–1,600**

A scarce Sowerby dolphin bowl in *blanc-de-lait* glass, c.1890, **$960–1,280**

▼ The cow with the iron tail

This three-footed bowl design, produced by Sowerby from 1880s molds, survived to the late 1920s. It was also made in clear and amber, and in a shiny opaque glass, called "vitro-porcelain", in the now rare Esthetic green and yellow. There were many shape variations, formed from the still warm, pressed as round, glass form. The fiery-opal, bone-ash effect seen here was not unique to Sowerby, but the company was praised at the time for the "milk in water" effect, with one commentator amusingly referring to it as the "cow with the iron tail."

▼ Baskets

The nostalgic, rustic appeal of baskets dates from the 18thC, with porcelain flowers overflowing from trugs and baskets in all manner of designs. The essentially urban 19thC wallowed in ruralism, especially during the peak of the influence of the Morris group, from the 1870s. The basket appears in countless variations in pressed glass, and whole collections of only this exist. Sometimes found with imitation willow, or rush weaving, the baskets are mostly floral in design, with imitation cut-glass patterns also common. The Davidson's example shown below was possibly intended for the display of small flowers, such as primroses and violets.

An ornamental basket in blue "Pearline", by Davidson, c.1890, **$64–96**

▼ Novelty fusions

The item shown below is of uncertain origin. The bowl, in clear, blue glass, and the stand, in amber, were separately pressed and fused together. This novelty also exists with an amber top and a blue base, and was probably sold with its partner as a disparate pair. The bowl has a fancy open edge, and bears a design of swans and river plants. The support is from a very complex mold, which was probably German made; the glass could have been Belgian or French.

A novelty, duotone fancy bowl and integral stand, of uncertain origin, c.1895, **$56–72**; a reverse pair **$160–200**

Novelties

Superb examples of unusual shapes and rare colors from unknown sources exist, and prices are generally moderate. Collecting offbeat and unusual colors can be rewarding, and could lead to a study of colored-glass technology. All open-ended collections are invaluable contributions to the unfinished history of glass. All you need are patience and a long-term view.

▼ Vivid colors

Each color used for pressing glass needs a separate melting pot which must be re-used only for that color. A pot can, however, be used to produce a tint that another suitable color mixture might produce from any residue, and there are superb examples of rich, unusual colors, such as the vivid green-blue seen on the basket below. Another feature of this basket is the looped handle, which was integrally molded with the basket, representing a technical advance in mold-making.

An ornamental basket of unknown origin, early 1900s, **$72–104**

Mugs & cups

The late 18th and early 19thC name for a coffee mug was a can. In 19thC glass manufacturers' catalogs, mugs were sometimes referred to as cans, but the word "mug" became more common toward the end of the century. None of the items shown here is in heat-proof glass, which appears only from the early 1920s in practical oven ware; it wasn't until the 1930s that thin, toughened glass was perfected, allowing the manufacture of glass teapots, cups, and table plates. Most fancy-glass mugs, cups, and saucers were, therefore, novelties, and would have been bought for the simple reason that they had not been seen before. Today they are a collector's delight, and are much sought after.

▼ Every one different

The cup-and-saucer set shown here has extraordinarily fluid streaking on the saucer, and more restrained marbling on the cup. While one gather of glass is usually squeezed in a mold, this type of glass required two blobs of glass, one opaque purple and the other opaque white, and the molding pressure produced unpredictable, random marbling. Most multiple pieces don't match, and really outlandish streaking adds value to items.

Cup and saucer by Sowerby, in marbled slag glass, early 1880s,
$240–320

▶ Novelty gift mugs

Evidence that marbled mugs were novelties or gift ware is manifest in this Sowerby slag mug from around 1890. There is a pattern of ivy and berries, but the texture of the glass makes this difficult to read. Opposite the handle is a panel that reads "A Present From" with, in this case, a blank panel underneath. There were two ways of customizing this mug: the mold had a replaceable section, into which a name could be cut, or the retailer could paint a name onto the blank area. It is more than possible that this example once bore a cold-painted town or area name, which has simply worn off.

A Sowerby "A Present From" slag-glass mug, c.1890,
$144–216

A Greener, Sunderland, cobalt-blue mug, c.1895, **$96–128**

▲ Bristol blue?

This beautiful, translucent, rich blue mug, with rustic twig handles, has a finely molded design of wheat and cornflowers. Cobalt blue was one of the most appealing glass colors; it was seen as therapeutic in the 1880s, with several "scientists" declaring blue glass to be calming and attractive to certified lunatics. The color is linked to Bristol because the necessary cobalt ore, or zaffre, was imported to the U.K. through that port. Blue glass was made there, of course, but also practically everywhere else. It appears as a colorant for pressed glass from the early 19thC, and is still very popular indeed.

▼ Swan song

The curious, pressed mug below is unmarked, but analysis of the design can provide clues to its provenance. The "riveted" handle is copied from "old" metalwork; there are architectural references in the surmounting and pendant spheres; and the swans are very prominent. All this is romantically 19thC, apart from the plain, horizontal nature of the base and the rim: very 1930s. There was a 1930s nationalistic revival of interest in Germany in the Wagner-inspired follies of King Ludwig II of Bavaria, especially Neuschwanstein. In German, *Stein* can mean stone (hence New Swanstone) or a mug of some description. This mug is a delightful pun in German: new (*Neu*) swan (*Schwan*) mug (*Stein*).

An unusual, amber swan mug, 1930s, German or Czech, **$64–80**

Glass mugs & cups

Collecting molded glass in shapes that are theoretically utilitarian is different from collecting ostensibly decorative items. There is a satisfaction in the variety of cup or mug shapes, as well the fun of finding a familiar form in an unfamiliar color. Be canny and collect both glass and china cups, saucers, and mugs: new relationships may be revealed.

FACT FILE

A green, U.S. Depression Glass cup and saucer, late 1930s, **$24–32**

▲ Depression Glass

Machine-produced glass was sold amazingly cheaply from the 1930s to the 1950s. Huge matching services were made, with everything from butter-dishes to salt-shakers, which ensured consumer come-back, even during the Depression. This glass still looks good on modern tables, and is avidly collected in the U.S.A. It is found throughout Europe, but not in vast quantities. Some popular designs have been reproduced.

Vases

The greatest variety of shape, size, and decoration in molded popular glass can be found within the very catholic canon of the "vase". The designers, mostly unknown, raided every source they could find, and the result is a veritable *embarras de richesses*. Vase mold-makers excelled themselves with complex molds, reaching a peak of artistic achievement in the late 19thC; many of these molds were used well into the 20thC. Some of the largest vases were made by U.S. Carnival Glass factories from 1910 to 1925. The geometric, machine look of the 1920s and 1930s is also reflected in contemporary molded vases.

▼ Esthetic swans

This beguiling vase, in an opaque vitro-porcelain, was pressed by Sowerby. It is in giallo, or Esthetic yellow, as it is called by modern commentators. This offbeat color is certainly linked to what Gilbert & Sullivan parodied as the "greenery-yallery, Grosvenor Gallery" period of Esthetic adventure, and its rather precious search for "beauty." The formality of the swans in this case recalls French Empire Neo-classicism of 1805–1814, and the influence of Morris is not far away in the naturalistic depiction of the rushes. The mold itself is a *tour de force* of great precision, and was probably made of brass or gunmetal rather than the usual fine iron.

An exceptional swan vase by Sowerby, in yellow vitro-porcelain, late 1880s, **$800–1,040**

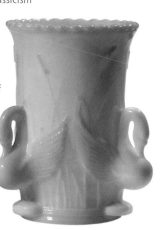

A "Chipanese" chimneypiece vase, in white vitro-porcelain by Sowerby, 1890s, **$120–160**

◀ "Chipanese" style

Throughout the 19thC, British manufacturing industry reflected the interest in the Orient by producing goods that were decorated in a Chinese/Japanese manner, producing a style called "Chipanese". Certainly there was a popular craze for all things Japanese during the 1880s and 1890s. As Japan was an integral part of Estheticism it is no surprise to see novelties, such as this item from Sowerby, especially as John George Sowerby himself published an "Esthetic" children's book in 1880, and another in 1881, both of which recalled the work of Kate Greenaway.

An eclectic vase, by Davidson, in black purple, c.1890, **$160–240**

▲ The jet set

Black glass is said to be the kiss of death in the glass trade. It is made by adding to the glass quantities of manganese, which produces a darkness that does not readily transmit light, but can be seen as deep purple with a strong light. Genuine jet-black glass, often used for "jet" buttons, was made by adding iron filings, as a blackening contaminant, to the glass mixture before it was melted. Davidson's black vase shown above is highly eclectic – a base of three lions, bearing escutcheons, is linked by floral swags, and a running band of Greek-key design. Gothic panels enclose roses, thistles and shamrocks. Wales is not included.

▼ Nosegays and funerals

The two Carnival Glass vases shown below represent the huge variety of size that was available in this type of glass during its heyday in the U.S.A. The tiny, ribbed "Morning Glory" vase, with a smoke finish, was made by Imperial Glass, and the large "Rustic" vase, with a golden marigold coating, by The Fenton Art Glass Company. The very large vases have become known by collectors in the U.S.A. as "funeral vases." These large, spectacular vases are much sought after.

A small, Imperial vase, in unusual smoke color, **$48–80**; a "funeral vase" by Fenton in marigold, **$400–800**

Cloud Glass

There have been attempts, mostly by keen dealers, to arouse interest in certain types of popular glass, such as Cloud Glass. If it interests you, buy it now while you can, as it is fairly reasonably priced. This type of glass represents mechanical perfection; take care to avoid chips or cracks, because pieces of this cleanly molded glass must be in mint condition to justify and maintain their value.

▼ Top-class Cloud Glass

The 1925 Paris Exhibition displayed luxury goods, including the dense, richly textured *pâte-de-verre* produced by packing molds with ground-down and powdered colored glass. The firing to fuse the crushed glass was tricky, as was the subsequent cooling, but the result was an expensive, thick, heavy glass, streaked and mottled with the depth of semi-precious stones. Davidson emulated this look, using subtly colored versions of "slag" glass. It was called "Cloud Glass," and was a great hit in the 1930s.

A 1930s, "tortoiseshell", Cloud Glass vase by Davidson, **$320–480**

Lighting

When mass production of molded glassware began, in the 1820s, domestic lighting was by oil lamps or candles. Many molded fancy bases for metal and glass oil lamps, fitted with brass wicks and chimney galleries, and dating from the 1830s, exist; some are still being made and used today. The most attractive lighting item to the modern collector, however, is the candlestick. Tall sticks made sure that light would be well distributed when they were placed on tables, which is where most were used; short examples are chamber sticks, and would have functioned as personal lighting from hall to bedroom. All are decorative, as well as functional, reflecting the fact that they were necessities. As attractive and readily available collectibles they fit nicely on to shelves, and can be used for special occasions when candlelight is wanted, to flatter and allure.

A Sowerby, "Queen's Ware" candlestick, c.1885, **$320–400**

◀ Queen Ann and "Queen's Ware"

This Sowerby candlestick from the early 1880s is unusual in bearing on the base the mark of the retailer for whom it was specially manufactured: "Queen Ann Candlestick. J. Mortlock & Co., Oxford & Orchard St., London." Mortlock sold china and glass, and commissioned many such items. This glass candlestick is based on an 18thC silver item, later copied in Leeds creamware, and reproduced by Worcester in porcelain around 1875. Sowerby probably borrowed the latter version, using cream vitro-porcelain in a color it called "Queen's Ware." This is a unique example of multiple plagiarism.

▼ Fairy Lights and pyramids

Table lighting using fashionable shaded candles was problematic – the shades often caught fire, and the candles often collapsed. By controlling quality, and supplying suitable devices, Samuel Clark introduced the small, cased, long-burning "Fairy Light" candles. Many firms supplied the upper shades for Clark's patent pressed bases. These shades could be hand-made or pressed, as are these examples.

Two 1880s "Fairy Lights" complete with shades, **$160–480** each

▼ Sowerby candlestick

First made in the 1880s, the Sowerby candlestick below was still in production well into the 20thC. As with the Queen Ann example, there is a complex series of decorative quotations fused into one highly eclectic structure. The twisting, Salomonic column is surmounted by a capital of indeterminate order. It rests on a base with smooth egg-and-dart decoration, as well as some Rococo "C" scrolls arranged as a Gothic trefoil. This really is an object lesson in the design confusion of the last quarter of the 19thC, as this piece would have matched exactly the confused décor in which it was intended to be used.

A Sowerby, Carnival Glass candlestick, **$400–480**, with matching chamber stick, **$160–240**, both in jet glass, c.1928

▲ "Rainbo Lustre"

Sowerby iridized a great deal of its pressed glass from about 1924 to 1939. This output commenced as U.S. Carnival Glass production faded, leaving the overseas demand an open market. These lighting devices are pressed in dense, black, jet glass, as were some similarly plain, geometric vases of the same period. The dark spray used on them produces a finish called "Rainbo Lustre" – hoping to appear "Yankee." Sowerby called the golden marigold "Sunglow." There is a strong and rising demand for inter-war Carnival Glass made in Scandinavia and England, and on the Continent. Black examples are scarce and valuable.

An elaborately patterned, Sowerby vitro-porcelain candlestick, 1880s, **$144–192**

Collecting tip

Now is the time to buy glass Fairy Lights, candlesticks, and candelabra while prices are low. Snap up any bargains, especially anything in pairs, which are worth much more than the sum of two individuals. Clark's Fairy Lights are a must; any complete multi-Fairy-Light fixture is valuable, but all the shades must match.

A rare Czech candelabrum, with titanium iridescence, c.1937, **$960–1,280**

▲ Czechoslovakia

From 1919, the new Republic of Czechoslovakia expanded its already large glass and costume-jewellery industry in Bohemia. By the 1930s, when the candelabrum above was made, new technology made innovative colors of metallic luster possible. The brilliant, thin-film luster evident here was from titanium.

For the dressing-table

Suburban expansion in the U.K. in the late 1920s and the 1930s gave rise to mock-Tudor terraces, and semi-detached dream houses, with bay windows providing the illusion of space and healthy light. The ladies-only triple-mirrored dressing-table went into this luminous bay, and was smothered with knick-knacks and the repertoire of beauty maintenance. Glass dressing-table-set production boomed in the inter-war years: a brush-and-comb tray, two candlesticks, and two or three lidded bowls were standard. Further matching items, such as cologne bottles, perfume atomizers, hair-pin trays, and ring stands, were also produced. Other items present in the boudoir were often empty, attractive cosmetics packaging.

▶ **Tray and candlesticks**
The seaside piers of Britain supported many small theaters that between the wars played summer shows with the "Pierrot Concert Parties", and attendant Pierrettes. This period is evoked by the part dressing-table set of the early 1930s shown here. The tray depicts Pierrette fanning herself, while Pierrot serenades her. The candlesticks are also musical: the girl coyly observes the boy strumming his instrument. The escapist, romantic appeal of such sets is immense. Other sets have butterflies, birds, and jazzy, geometric designs. Plain sets are not as popular.

An anonymous, early 1930s dressing-table set with superb narrative decoration; complete set (with covered bowls) **$800–960**

▼ **Bohemian staining and flashing**
From the early 19thC, much Bohemian glass was multi-layered, to create designs and patterns by being selectively cut through. Cased glass is successive layers of glass; if the overlay glass is very thin, it is called flashing. This 1930s press-molded dressing-table lidded bowl has, however, been selectively stained by brushing. Silver nitrate gives a translucent, amber coating, as seen here, when re-heated. Although this item is not cut, it gives the impression of having been produced by a double-layered cutting process.

A Czech, silver-stained, pressed-glass dressing-table item, part of a set, 1930s, **$56–72**, complete set **$320–400**

▼ Red Cloud

Davidson enjoyed a huge success with its Cloud Glass. The angular, red, covered powder bowl below recalls Oriental lacquer techniques, which was deliberate. This early example has original Davidson's paper labels, giving both a patent number (329022), and the date (1929). The exterior effect is superb. It was created by brushing or spraying the interior of the bowl with a red paint. The base color, a thin tortoiseshell effect, can be clearly seen on the finial. Technically, pressed red glass was economically viable by the late 1920s, but not with the streaky "Cloud" effect seen here. This is a scarce color effect in Cloud Glass, and is in increasing demand.

A rare, red, fully labelled, Davidson's Cloud Glass powder bowl, dated 1929, **$560–720**

A Czech, Carnival Glass "Origami" dressing-table set (only one large lidded jar shown), complete set in marigold **$240–280**

▲ "Origami"

This is a good example of the many 1930s, geometric dressing-table sets. It is known to Carnival Glass collectors, who assign identification names to all designs, as "Origami." As well as marigold, these sets can be found in clear blues, greens, and pinks. Some are acid-sprayed or sand-blasted to matte finishes. They are not as sought after as either the figural, narrative items, or those displaying flora and fauna, but they do show the clean, geometrical angularities, made from molds that required no actual artistic skills, used on pressed glass during the austere 1930s.

▼ Fragrant clouds

Atomizers were a development of the refined manufacturing processes developed for rubber during World War I. The principal company to market brass spray heads was de Vilbis, which also issued its own complete atomizers. The rubber bulbs and tubing were unpleasant to touch, and were generally covered in silk. These will have now perished, but they can be replaced.

A de Vilbis iridescent perfume atomizer, c.1925, with replacement bulb, tubing, and silk covering, **$80–96**

Slag glass

The former close proximity of the coal, coke, iron, and steel industries to the pressed-glass factories of north-eastern England resulted in close relationships. "Slag" is a name given to vitrified cinders, as well as to scum floating on molten metal, and this ingredient was included in glass both as a bulking agent, and to render it opaque. It was cheap, and available locally, and was used during the 1880–1900 fad for marbled glass. Inconsistency, however, led to slag being abandoned. Various opaque mixtures of glass, when squeezed together in a mold, produce the marbled effect now incorrectly called slag.

▼ Marbled dairy dishes

U.K. factories using marbled "malachite" glass include Sowerby, Davidson, and Greener. It was also used in the U.S.A. As it became popular in the 1880s, all manner of molds were used for its production. It is now clear that some items, usually plain and simple pieces, are relatively common, while others are rarely found. This cow butter-dish was originally issued in clear glass, so that the butter could be seen; the opaque slag-glass version unfortunately met consumer resistance.

A rare, Davidson "cow" figural covered butter-dish, in purple and white slag glass, 1885, **$960–1,200**

▶ Camouflage

At first glance, it is not apparent that this stemmed, covered sugar and cream jug were intended to be a pair, and bear the same design. As they have been pressed from "malachite" glass, the eye has been totally confused. Slag glass was often called "malachite" glass, irrespective of its color. It looks best when plainly moulded, but the decorative plurality of the age in which it was used left few molds unadorned. This set would have seen little service on the table; it would have been used if it had been in clear glass. Rather like a lavish cup and saucer, it would have gone straight into the display cabinet.

A covered sugar, and matching creamer, of uncertain origin, in greeny-blue slag glass, 1880–95, set **$320–480**

Offbeat slag

Rarities can include a familiar shape with a one-off decoration, or they can represent a technical experiment. An offbeat slag piece, displaying odd marbling, is of greater interest than the piece in clear glass. Not all rarities are expensive, as they can be unrecognized and undervalued.

▼ Spill vases galore

One of the great successes of pressed-glass marketing was the vase of a sufficient height and diameter to hold spills neatly on the chimneypiece. It could, of course, have been used for other purposes, but that was its primary function. The spill vase shown below is another example of the eclectic ideas of the 1880s. The cylindrical vase rests on flared, classical lappets, with anthemion decoration. A band of Maltese crosses leads to a plain area, followed by a band of strapworked, pendant, Gothic trefoils. All is surmounted by a scalloped rim with a band of chained circles that frame round bosses. The rare, olive-green slag glass is as remarkable as the design.

A rare, olive-green slag-glass spill vase, of complex design, maker uncertain, 1880s, **$400–480**

A blue, slag-glass, Sowerby flower boat, 1890s, **$200–280**

▲ Moss-filled boats and troughs

Grim, late-Victorian, U.K. cities wallowed in sulphurous soot and smoke. Middle- and upper-working-class houses tried to alleviate this squalor with aspidistras (one of the few house plants tough enough to survive), silk, wax, and paper flowers, and precious seasonal posies. Those with the means embellished dining-tables with flower boats, and low troughs of posies. The Sowerby boat above was from an existing mold borrowed from pattern number 1874, a clear-glass table service issued in 1884. It would have been filled with moss, greenery, and flowers. There are a smaller and a larger version.

A very rare, gray, slag spill vase, probably Sowerby, late 1870s– early 1880s, **$1,280–1,440**

▲ Real slag?

The extraordinary, gray color of this unmarked vase is early, and is probably derived from the use of industrial, vitrified slag. If it were to fracture, there is no doubt where this vase would split. It is not an attractive color, so was surely accidental or experimental. The mold is crisp, clean, and precise, and was obviously new. Evidence indicates it is a Sowerby mold.

Opalescent glass

The opal gemstone displays milky-blue opaqueness one moment, and deep fiery depths the next. The same effect characterizes glass that has had phosphate added to the mix. Pre-1930s this was in the form of powdered, calcined animal bones, but this was then replaced by the precisely formulated chemical phosphates, alumina and fluorine. This fiery glass was used in Venice, and appears in U.S. pressed glass from around the 1830s. If glass of a uniform thickness was used, an even opalescent effect was produced, and was called "opaline." Press-molded glass varies in profile thickness, and the thicker sections display effects of a thick, intense, milky blue that presents a pale orange, fiery, opalescent quality when held to the light.

▲ Pikes and troughs from Manchester

Elegant table-settings were satisfactory only if they were novel during the last quarter of the 19thC. Themes were popular, and nautical ideas, for example, were supplied in silver, ceramics, and glass. The Manchester firm of Molineaux, Webb & Co. created a pike design, registered in 1885, in two sizes, of which this is the smaller (see p.54), in fiery, opalescent glass. It was intended for a table arrangement of flowers, and matched the 10" table centre example.

A Manchester, opalescent posy-trough, in the form of a pike, c.1890, **$240–320**

A Manchester, opalescent canoe, with integrally molded, rustic trunk supports, c.1885, **$320–480**

▼ Hearts of oak

This English canoe shape, from Burtles & Tate, Manchester, was registered in 1885, and is decorated with oak leaves and acorns. The rustication feature in the supporting trunks is found on much pressed glass. Many similar boats, of many sizes, were made, but they are scarce in opalescent glass. This type of glass follows on in the 1890s from the 1870s–80s slag glass, which was often referred to as "malachite." Opalescent glass, in blue and uranium yellow, was advertised by Davidson from 1889 as "Pearline."

▼ Lalique copies

There were many attempts to emulate the pre-war, opalescent Lalique look. Some bear the name or mark of the maker – look for Sabino, Ettling, Valux, Barolac, and Opalique. Other cheaper items are often simply light-blue glass, mostly frosted, depicting artistic nudes and animals. All are from the 1930s. Some have fake Lalique signatures, and some original marks have been ground out.

▼ Going for a swan

Variations of the basic opalescent effect were developed during the late 1880s. By mixing bone ash with cobalt blue and uranium oxide, Davidson was able to offer items in intensely highlighted, opalized blue "Pearline," and acidic yellow "Primrose Pearline," which remained in production for about 30 years from 1889. These colored "opals" gradually overtook the appeal of opaque slag production as the century closed. Manchester firms introduced rose-pink, highlighted opalescent effects, presumably by incorporating some form of copper into the bone ash. There was also "Sunset" opalescent, which was both pink, and a sallow uranium yellow. This swan was made in rose opalescent, by Burtles & Tate, from molds of designs registered in 1885.

A Manchester, opalescent rose swan trinket, Burtles & Tate, c.1890, **$400–480**

▼ Bird in a bush

This bird bowl is similar, with its acorns, oak leaves, and rusticated tree trunk, to the boat shown on the opposite page. It is obviously from the same mold-maker, and it is no stylistic surprise to find that it is another 1885 design registration of Burtles & Tate. The fiery, bone-ash opalescence is most intense within the thick sections of the bird and its tree-trunk support. Manchester-made glass is of a very high quality, and has an addictive variety of designs, and prices for it are reaching very serious levels indeed.

A Manchester opalescent bird bowl, Burtles & Tate, 1885, **$240–320**

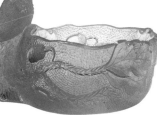

▼ Opalique or Lalique?

James Augustus Jobling took over the financially stricken Greener factory in Sunderland in 1885, and ran it as Greener's. As Jobling's, from 1921, it made a wide range of fancy glassware in the 1930s, but this was not profitable. Much of it was based on the Lalique look, and was made in opalescent glass, boldly using the mark "Opalique." The Fir Cone, no. 777133, was the first pattern to be registered, in 1932, and was also made in other colors, such as pink and blue.

A Jobling, "Opalique" fir-cone bowl, c.1935, **$320–400**

Carnival Glass

Glass with a metallic luster finish was particularly popular in Europe and the U.S.A. around 1900. The production process used cheap metallic salts, that were sprayed or selectively applied to iridize the surface of the glass. High-class use of this technique includes the art glass of L. C. Tiffany, in the U.S.A. and Lötz Witwe in Austria-Hungary. Mass-produced, molded glass with this iridescent surface started to appear in the U.S.A. from 1905. It was widely exported, was eventually manufactured around the world, and is still in production today. It was attractive, and democratically priced, and the market rose in the period leading up to World War I, as the allure of the similar art glass sank.

▼ Northwood

Harry Northwood, son of the 19thC English art-glassmaker John Northwood, ran his factory in West Virginia, where molded ware was given an additional iridescent coating as the fad grew in the early 20thC. Northwood marked almost all of his glass with an "N" in a circle (see p.60). This excellent fruit bowl is finely pressed, and hand-crimped, and is a good example of quality Carnival Glass made from c.1909 to 1919.

A cobalt-blue, Grape & Cable, three-footed bowl, Northwood, U.S.A., c.1910, **$320–640**

▼ Grape & Cable pattern

The hatpin vanished as the aerodynamic hats of pre-World War I gave way to head-clinging, flapper cloches. Iridized hatpin heads and fashion buttons came from the myriad small glass-jewellery factories around Gablonz, in Bohemia, from 1890 to 1914. This hatpin holder is the same Grape & Cable design as the adjacent footed bowl. Northwood had a vast range of matching goods in this pattern. Other factories, notably Fenton, produced limited and imitative versions.

A purple-glass hatpin holder, Northwood, c.1910, **$320–640**, and two Bohemian hatpins of the same date, **$80–120**

Collecting tip
Carnival Glass is a very popular collectible, with ever-rising prices – a general collection is now not possible, so new collectors should specialize in one aspect. Plates are very expensive, as are some colors, such as red, but tumblers with rare patterns are constantly surfacing. Buy what bargains you can, and trade to improve.

A Broken Arches punch-bowl on stand with 12 cups, Imperial Glass, U.S.A., c.1920; complete set **$800–1,600**, depending on color. This marigold is the cheapest

▲ Imperial splendour
Imperial Glass, now defunct, was located at Bellaire, Ohio. The factory made its name with "Nucut" pressed glass, made to replicate the sparkling intricacies of brilliant, turn-of-the-century cut glass. Much of this was iridized, and this punch set represents the popularity of these ostentatious items. Imperial Carnival Glass was made in clear, purple, and green glass, as well as small quantities, now scarce, of blue and red. The color shown is called marigold by collectors, but was marketed as "Rubigold." Most early U.S. Carnival Glass factories made a variety of punch sets; prices are generally higher for the scarcer, darker colors and opalescent finishes.

A two-handled, Mary Anne vase in purple, by Dugan/Diamond Glass, U.S.A., c.1914, **$120–240**

▲ The Dugan/Diamond Glass Company
Many novelty vases exist in Carnival Glass. This simple and functionally obvious "loving-cup" vase, also produced with three handles, was made by the factory that was initially operated by Thomas Dugan. It became Diamond Glass, until it was destroyed by fire in 1931, and made general Carnival Glass, and also clear glass, with opalescent edging and highlights.

▼ Virtuoso mold-cutting
Carnival Glass abounds in spectacular designs. The Imperial "Nu-Art" Homestead plate shown below dates from the early 1920s. It has a Greek-key border, which it shares with its companion plate depicting chrysanthemums. Other patterns often combine surprising elements in a curious or naive manner. Prices are now governed by speculative collectors, who are mostly also the top dealers.

A purple, Imperial "Nu-Art" Homestead, Carnival Glass plate, 1920s, **$1,600–3,200**

▼ Fenton

The Fenton Art Glass Company introduced a full range of iridized, pressed glass from 1907, inaugurating one of the most popular types of molded glass ever made. The Fenton family factory, still flourishing in West Virginia, must be given the accolade for popularizing Carnival Glass. Fenton introduced economically viable, pressed red glass, a technical breakthrough, as a base color in the 1920s, as demand for Carnival Glass was on the wane in the U.S.A. The small, three-footed bowl below is from the mold for a small dish from a fruit set. Early red items by Fenton are scarce, and sought after.

A Fenton, crimped, three-footed, small, red, Panther bowl, mid-1920s, **$960–1,600**

▼ Unusual colors

The Fenton factory produced many curious patterns, as well as fascinating, short runs of unusual base colors. Together with variants of hand-shaping of molded items, this has created a collector's paradise. Other factories also produced limited, iridized versions of novelty colors or pastel shades, often with frosty or opalescent finishes. Uranium glass, opaque white glass, semi-translucent blue and green glass, and marbled glass, sometimes resembling tortoiseshell, were also iridized, albeit rarely. The small, stemmed comport below by Fenton was molded in uranium glass, often called vaseline (see p.45).

▼ Worldwide production

While U.S. production of Carnival Glass faded away in the mid-1920s, other countries made it to supply local demand from the early 1920s to 1939. The butter-dish below was made in Germany, in the late 1920s to early 1930s, by the Brockwitz factory. At this time Sowerby was re-using surviving 19thC molds; Crown Crystal in Sydney cut indigenous flora and fauna molds in an early, splendid outburst of Australian identity, and other factories in France, Belgium, Italy, Czechoslovakia, Finland, Sweden, Argentina, and India also made Carnival Glass in the years up to 1939, often using German molds.

A blue, lidded, Rose Garden butter-dish by Brockwitz, c.1929, **$800–1,200**

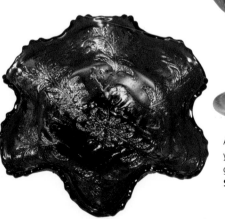

A small, Holly comport, in yellow uranium "vaseline" glass, by Fenton, c.1916, **$80–96**

Carnival glass

What does the name mean? In the 1950s, dealers wishing to rehabilitate iridescent art-glass prices called this puzzling product Carnival Glass. This unfortunate generic name has stuck, but is totally incorrect. It is also often called "Poorman's Tiffany."

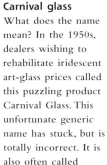

▼ Reproductions

From the 1960s, collectors worldwide, initially in the U.S.A., became enthused by the vast amounts of Carnival Glass available. So began imaginative and speculative documentation, which owed more to creative thinking than to scholarly appraisal. Added to this enthusiastic "guidance" was reproduction Carnival Glass, which appealed to a new generation of innocent collectors. Imperial was able to reproduce its past. Fenton, as well as reproducing its own Carnival Glass, was also using molds purchased from defunct factories of former rivals. The butter-dish shown below is a marigold item made by Imperial in the 1970s from old, 19thC, American molds.

Covered butter-dish, c.1975, by Imperial from old molds, **$280–360**

▼ New versus old

The tumbler shown below was made from an old mold that was not originally used for the production of Carnival Glass. Attractive items constantly appear, and there are several categories to be aware of: old Carnival Glass made in the U.S.A., 1905–1929; secondary production made outside the U.S.A. from 1924 to 1939; reproduction ware made from the 1960s, using original molds; new Carnival Glass, using old molds not made for iridescent goods; and new items made from specially cut molds.

A new, Carnival Glass tumbler from an old mold called "Holly-Agate", 1960s, **$80–112**

▼ Souvenirs and limited-edition memorabilia

Many worldwide Carnival Glass organizations issue souvenirs bearing the name of the group. Below is a red-glass, handled bell, made for the Heart of America Carnival Glass Association (HOACGA), and a blue plate, Peacock & Dahlia, issued to celebrate the 15th anniversary of the Carnival Glass Society (U.K.).

Left to right: small, blue plate and red-glass, handled bell, both by Fenton, c.1990, **$80–96**

Decorated wares

Popular, molded glassware is usually found as it was made, without any fancy coloring or special effects, but much of it, including simple, mold-blown forms, was originally decorated, using a variety of techniques. Cold-painted decoration, particularly used by the French Vallerysthal factory, has today mostly worn off, which gives pieces a rather dishevelled appearance. Gilding was rarely used, but it is sometimes found. Permanent fired-on enameling was uncommon, and appears mostly on small, Sowerby items. Bohemia produced plain, small items that were either enameled or decorated with fine, glass granules.

A blue, vitro-porcelain vase with very rare gilding, probably Sowerby, 1880s, **$480–560**

▶ **Gilding**
This design is not one of the most elegant of the 19thC (see also p.35). The attempt to produce a trio of classical gryphons – the body of a lion, with the wings and beak of an eagle – has failed, although the fur-to-feather fusion was well handled in the mold-cutting. The fine gilding is carefully applied to the chain and neck rings, as well as in a line under the truncated fluting of the rim. It is fascinating that the sophisticated Classicism of this selectively decorated item emphasizes special "gold" chains, which warn that the transmogrified "swans" are divinities of supernatural form.

▼ **Hot enameling**
While paint is a pigment, suspended in a medium suitable for cold application, enamel is ground-up glass in an oily medium, that needs heat to fuse the colored, powdered glass permanently to the surface to which it has been applied. Sowerby used unskilled labour for this simple work. The single color used on the items below is warm sepia, applied to the panel borders and the Baroque flourish.

A scarce, enameled cream-and-sugar set in white vitro-porcelain, Sowerby, 1880s, set **$400–480**

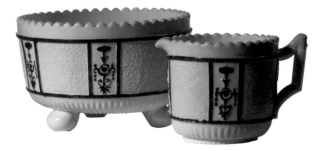

An advertising ashtray for cigarettes, reverse transfer printed, 1930s, **$56–80**

A Fenton, enameled, cobalt-blue, Carnival Glass water set, *c*.1914; pitcher **$960–1,040**, tumblers **$112–144** each

▲ Decorated Carnival Glass

The enameled set above is called "Forget-me-not" by collectors. The pattern was painted in-house at the Fenton Art Glass Factory by teams of women, and there is a fluency about the brushwork that recalls barge decoration or European folk art. This is true enamel fired onto the glass. The pitcher's handle is not iridized; it would have been applied by hand after the molded body had been sprayed. Many other Carnival Glass pitchers have a similar construction. Northwood and Dugan also issued enameled Carnival Glass in the U.S.A., but such decoration ceased during World War I.

▲ Advertising

Ashtrays such as this were given to public houses, bars, and restaurants as part of tobacco brand-marketing. These cheaply pressed items were transfer-printed on the rear, and sealed with gold paint. This decoration lasted quite well, but eventually it flaked and wore away, as can be seen here. Publicans simply dunked the ashtrays in paint stripper when they became too worn and re-used them plain. Items such as this are difficult to find in anything like mint condition, and pristine examples are valuable. Whisky and rum also featured on similar ashtrays, as did almost every brewery and beer.

▼ Beading, jeweling and coral

Simply molded, small vases and flasks were mass-produced in Bohemia, where most were mold-blown via alder-wood molds. Small workshops bought blanks and decorated them, principally for export, in unusual, and impulsively desirable, techniques. Complex enameling is quite common, but rarer items are decorated with fused beads and glass jewels at appropriate points. Fine glass granules were fused on to items in coral and seaweed designs. A coral example is shown here.

A rare, small, blow-molded and coral-decorated novelty vase, Bohemia, *c*.1900–1914, **$64–80**

Swans

Swans are a symbolic part of many religious beliefs, and figure in associated texts and mythology, generally linking the powerful elements of air and water. Swans represent goodness, purity, and, above all, love. Christians soon transferred associations of the swan to the Virgin Mary; Hindu belief has two unified swans, representing a heavenly union toward which all heavenly beings must fly; Brahma was born from the cosmic, golden egg of a swan; and in China it is a yang bird linked to the sun.

The swan became an apparent part of the 19thC decorative language from its use by, and association with, the French Empire style and the Empress Josephine. Pressed-glass swans need complex molds, and most factories produced at least one in order to maintain peer status. They have always sold well.

▼ Stourbridge swans
Little pressed glass is associated with the Stourbridge area of the U.K., which is still a bastion of traditional, hand-crafted glassware. This pressed-glass swan is one of a batch of designs registered by "Jane Webb & Joseph Hammond, trading as the executors of the late Joseph Webb, Stourbridge," in 1872–3. The moulds passed to Edward Moore at South Shields in 1888. This example is an early Stourbridge one, being crisply and precisely pressed from a tight, new mold. Later versions show oozy seams, and a slight overall blur.

An acid-obscured, pressed-glass swan, Stourbridge, c.1875, **$240–280**

▼ Double swans
In 1882 Sowerby issued a fine pattern book, number IX, in which this piece is listed as no. 1828. The design is very close to the 1877 Walter Crane frieze wallpaper "Swan, Rush and Iris." The finely cut mold, probably of refined bronze, has clever open areas, and it had a long life. Shown here in Esthetic green, it was last made in the late 1920s in "Sunglow" Carnival Glass, examples of which are now very rare indeed. This item is, in fact, desirable in any color.

A scarce, Esthetic-green Sowerby double-swan vase, c.1880, **$560–640**

Quality molds

Look for swans of quality, with evidence of bravura mold-making. Gaps between neck and wings are quite tricky. Also difficult are revealed, projecting webbed feet at the rear. Beaks and necks that are molded to the breast, with an air gap in between, are very advanced. Standing swans with open, worked legs are also difficult to cut as molds.

▼ Vaseline swan

Uranium appears as a glass colorant from Bohemian ores, in the 1830s, as either a yellow or a green, both of which are sharply acidic in tone. It was used intermittently through to the late 1930s when the ores became of interest for other, military, purposes. It gives off an unearthly, yellow glow when exposed to black ultra-violet light. It also clicks ominously when checked with a geiger counter. It is harmless, however, and should not be viewed with alarm. This lemon swan is of uranium glass, which has acquired the epithet "vaseline," resembling the emollient as it was, murkily greenish yellow, rather than the bland color it is now.

A uranium lemon "vaseline" glass swan, c.1890, **$96–120**

A U.S., Carnival Glass swan in sapphire blue, c.1912, **$240–320**

▲ Carnival swans

Many swans, and items with swan-derived decorative elements, were made in Europe, and by many U.S. glass companies, during the 19thC. They are particularly attractive in the metallic luster finishes used for Carnival Glass production. It is difficult to be precise with attribution, as many reproductions reusing old molds, as well as new Carnival Glass from new molds, confuse the situation. Swans also appear on molds for Carnival Glass dishes issued in the U.S.A. and Australia, and on iridized versions of the Sowerby covered butter-dish shown on p.17. Imperial Glass marketed very attractive swans in the 1970s; these are mold marked (see p.60), unlike old Imperial, which is not.

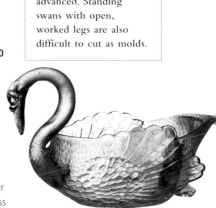

A large (15") U.S., molded swan in pink glass, late 1920s, **$1,120–1,280**

▲ The big swans

Cambridge Glass, Ohio, was famous for producing high-quality, pressed goods in attractive, often unique, colors. This pink, derived from selenium, dates from the late 1920s. Cambridge produced its famous swans in various sizes and colors, with the largest pressed-glass swan known pictured above. Any large swan which has survived intact is rare.

Other animals

Noah's Ark was not as rich in variety as the dazzling output of glass fauna produced in the U.S.A. and Europe during the 19thC! Cocks, hens, and chickens lead the way, usually nesting on butter-dish lids. Lids with assorted ducks, cows, swans, turkeys, squirrels, eagles, robins, boars' and bulls' heads, rabbits, lions, and dogs were also popular. Camels, owls, foxes, and sheep sometimes appeared on dish covers. Vallerysthal, the north-eastern French factory, produced large quantities of animal-covered dishes. Free-standing ornaments, in various sizes, were made featuring lions, dogs, and cats. Some animals, such as elephants, rarely appear, and are now very desirable. Many new and reproduction figural items exist (*see* p.56).

▼ A Turnbull hen

Covered hens still sell well when marketed. Mostly found on the "Covered Butters" pages of manufacturers' catalogs, they also appear as one-off items in the output of many smaller manufacturers. Such an example is shown below. Pressed in clear or flint glass, it was made by the Turnbull factory, Sunderland. Animal items from small, short-lived, poorly documented factories, such as Turnbull's, are keenly hunted for by canny collectors.

A press-moulded, clear-glass, covered hen by Matthew Turnbull, Sunderland, c.1890, **$160–240**

A Manchester, John Derbyshire lion ornament with crossed paws, 1873–76, **$240–280**

◄ The Landseer lions

The Manchester works of John Derbyshire operated from 1873 to 1876, when some superb glass designs were registered. The highly desirable Derbyshire glass includes lions (using the Landseer bronzes as inspiration, with parallel or crossed front paws), a whippet, a spectacular winged female, a Greek sphinx with diadem, figures of Punch and Judy (see p.51), and Britannia. Acid-matting of the glass is a characteristic of much Manchester work, and when used on black glass it gives an effect remarkably like Wedgwood's black basaltes. Molineaux, Webb & Co. issued an Egyptian sphinx (see p.51) from 1875.

Competition

Some collectors search for pressed-glass animals from one particular factory; others specialize in collecting pressed glass from certain areas, such as Manchester, and here too are desirable animal forms. Embarking on an animal collection is not cheap, but is fascinating. It may still be viable to collect animals, but prices are volatile; any available glass rapidly disappears.

▼ Whippets

The use of dogs in sporting activities is well known. Some sports are best forgotten, and coursing is one of them. It involved whippets chasing live hares to the death, and was a popular event in the northern U.K. industrial areas, which were nearly all bounded by suitable moors. It is recalled by the popular John Derbyshire chimneypiece ornament shown below. The keen-eyed whippet, a greyhound-terrier cross, poses patiently, and is depicted in an unusually lively manner. This is a fine example of popular glass truly recording social history, as well as demonstrating the history of taste.

A whippet "greyhound" ornament, in uranium "vaseline" glass, by John Derbyshire, 1873–76, **$320–400**

▼ Pink elephants

One of the great rarities of pressed glass is the pink elephant posy- or flower-holder of Burtles & Tate, Manchester. This highly attractive design, no. 64234, registered in 1886, is scarce in opal colors, and particularly rare in the rose opalescent shown below. The reason for this scarcity lies in the complexity of the mold; there must have been quite a few unsuccessful pressings. Known examples are crisp, but the problematic mold was soon abandoned for economic reasons.

A very rare, rose, opalescent elephant posy-holder, Burtles & Tate, Manchester, c.1886, **$3,200–4,800**

▼ Modern animals

There is currently a flourishing trade in the manufacture of pressed-glass novelties in the U.S.A. Many are zoomorphic, and the pig, or detusked boar, shown below, made by the Boyd company, is a late 20thC piece of pressed glass. This item is iridized, and is collected as new Carnival Glass (it is from a mold not originally used during the heyday of U.S. Carnival Glass, pre-1929). Reproduction Carnival Glass uses old molds or patterns that were made during this same period. The variety of glass used nowadays for these novelties is astonishing.

A new, Carnival Glass pig novelty, solid blue glass, Boyd, U.S.A., **$32–48**

Commemorative & souvenir wares

The 19thC was the century of progress, and historic and social events were faithfully recorded in the popular glass of the period in the U.K. Each new type of glass that came along was used on commemorative ware, along with new decorative techniques involving photography and transfer printing. Lettered, and often dated, examples were also made in the U.S.A., throughout continental Europe, and in Scandinavia. These "souvenirs" are well-traveled, but they are easy to identify, even if only from the language, place, person, or event depicted. European flea markets are interesting places to find unusual lettered wares. These add serious interest, and significant weight, to any collection of this type.

▶ **Exhibition plates**
Such items are quite scarce, but this Glasgow Exhibition plate issued in 1888, probably made by a north-eastern England factory, is relatively easy to find. It is sometimes found with cold-applied, red, green, and gold paint on the back, which gives a curious effect from the front. This painted decoration can also be found on some U.S. pressed glass, and such reverse-painted glass is collected, mostly in the U.S.A., as "Goofus Glass." The Glasgow Exhibition took place one year before the giant Paris 1889 Eiffel Tower Exhibition, but there were still over 2000 international exhibitors. It was much visited, and was open from May to November.

A Glasgow 1888 Exhibition plate, **$96–120**

▼ **The British Empire**
British pressed glass had a huge market, as it included all parts of the Empire. Although indigenous glass industries grew, fancy glass was mostly imported from the U.K. by the various nations. King Edward VII was immensely popular during his short reign, and the Coronation of June 1902 is well commemorated in both glass and ceramics. It is not known for certain who made the clear-glass item shown below, but it was certainly aimed at the Empire, with the biggest markets clearly indicated.

An Empire Coronation plate of 1902, showing Edward VII and Queen Alexandra, **$80–96**

A rare, open-edged, milk-glass plate, with a fused photograph of King Edward VII, c.1902, **$160–240**

▲ Photo portraits

George Eastman introduced the Kodak camera, 100 exposures on a paper roll, in 1888. By 1900, taking snaps was a world-wide hobby, and photography was no longer a novelty. What were new, however, were processes to fix photographs, as opposed to negatives, on to glass and glazed ceramics. The front photo example shown above was either photographically darkroom-printed onto sensitive solutions, or an invisibly-glued, specially glazed print. It is unclear where it was made, but it is marked, on the back, with the King's name as well as "Patented Aug 20, 1901."

▼ Seaside trips

Davidson at Gateshead developed a steady business in photographic souvenir ware, which is typified by the photographically-derived, reverse-transfer print shown below. Affixed to the back of the glass, the print was translucent yet reasonably waterproof. Blue opaline was the favoured color, and this same "frame" plate can be found depicting various resorts other than the ever popular Blackpool, as well as pictures of Queen Victoria. Similar European resort and city examples were made in clear glass, and were often randomly highlighted with slivers of mother-of-pearl.

A blue "Pearline", photo-transfer souvenir plate, Davidson, c.1895–1910, **$64–96**

Pressed-glass paperweights, with photographic views, c.1895, **$32–80**

▲ Paperweights

Simply molded, oval, round, or rectangular paperweights, with inset sections for decoration, were made from 1880 to the 1920s. Early examples had acid-etched or sand-blasted advertising on the bases. Printed paper advertisements were also used. From about 1900, real photographs were used, and the paperweights were sold as souvenirs. Expect to find almost any tourist attraction or location on these.

Figures & busts

It was difficult for makers of popular glass to decide on the personality or event worth investing in. And an investment it was, as the molds necessary for mass production were expensive, even if a standard mold was used up to 100,000 times. Complex multipart molds were more problematic, of course, and portrait busts were a risky business, especially of politicians, with their tendency to resign or to lose favor. Royalty were a better bet during the 19thC, but by the time Edward VII came to the throne, the market for portrait busts in glass was mostly finished. Rare 20thC glass busts and representations are those of Hitler, Mussolini, Lenin, and Stalin. There are also fine examples of many European monarchs, as well as philanthropists, musicians, and poets.

A rare, part-frosted, figural bitters bottle depicting Stanley, c.1875
$400–480

▼ Dr Livingstone, I presume?

Henry M. Stanley made his famous remark on finding David Livingstone at Ujiji, in October 1871. The two men then explored the northern end of Lake Tanganyika, and the river Rusizi. This expedition caught the public imagination, and soon became legendary. Many corked figural bottles were made to hold bitters: very strong alcohol disguised as medicine, which was universally popular in the 19thC. Most were made in the U.S.A.; some are French, and the Stanley example shown left is similar to known French examples. It has been selectively, if not very neatly, sand-blasted to enhance the sculptural effect.

▶ Mr Gladstone

A famous Chancellor of the Exchequer in the U.K., Gladstone became frustrated in his attempts to abolish income tax, and abandon protectionism. He was a reforming Prime Minister in 1868–74 and 1880–5, with the more popular Disraeli, who died in 1881, in between. Gladstone was commemorated in this bust, and there is a similar one of Disraeli, which is much easier to find. Most of these busts are acid-frosted, which makes the whole representation easier to read.

A frosted bust of Mr Gladstone, c.1880, **$320–560**

▼ Punch and Judy

This highly desirable pair was made by the Manchester firm of John Derbyshire (see p.46). Although made in various colors, the versions pressed from uranium-yellow glass have emerged as the most sought after. They should ideally be a matching pair, but the green and yellow duo below is not unattractive. Both Mr Punch and the harridan Judy are suitably modeled, and both are as amusing today as when they were made. A matching, undamaged pair is worth 50% more than a single item, and any Derbyshire item in uranium glass is worth 50% more than the same form in other colors.

Punch and Judy by John Derbyshire, Manchester, c.1873, **$400–960** each

A superb, Manchester, pressed sphinx by Molineaux, Webb & Co., c.1875, **$2,240–3,200**

▲ The riddle of the sphinx

The black, pressed sphinx shown above was made from a design registered in 1875. It is a standard Egyptian sphinx, and was perhaps an attempt to move upmarket and broaden the appeal of press-molded glass. Reasonably priced when new, this is now an expensive item, and is hard to find. It would have been sold as a pair when new. John Derbyshire's black, winged sphinx is worth twice as much, if not more.

▼ Car mascots

It was Lalique who was responsible for the late 1920s–early '30s craze for glass mascots to be affixed to car hoods. These mascots were expensive, and they often had flickering lights under them. Cheaper, anonymous versions were made in the 1930s, mostly in Czechoslovakia, where the mascot shown below was probably made. It is not signed, but it has its original metal base for fitting where needed.

An elfin moth car mascot, probably Czech, c.1935, **$800–1,200**

Novelties

"Novelties constantly" was an overworked phrase in 19thC glass advertising, suggesting hordes of designers and technicians working overtime to supply factories with new molds. Once pressed glass ceased to be a novelty in its own right, this situation was a necessity, and, having created a consumer market for glass, makers had to move on from making purely practical items. There are hats, hands, shoes, slippers, and boots, as well as revamped small knick-knack shapes, in short runs of unusual colors and fancy effects. The variety of colour, shape, and form is as bewildering as the general eclecticism of the late Victorian world. Many items still surface, to delight the collector and puzzle the historian.

A John Derbyshire, Manchester, hand vase in "vaseline" glass, c.1874, **$640–720**

▶ Handy items

Decorative, severed hands were popular in the late 19thC, with a superb example covered in seaweed being made by Gallé in the late 1890s. At the popular level, there are ceramic hands holding fish and flowers, and vase forms of all shapes and sizes. Palm-upward glass hands were just as popular, for example as flat pin trays of either one hand or a pair. More common are upright hands holding flowers, as shown here, where the decoration for once indicates a suggested function. The Avon cosmetics company has produced an impressive range of glass packaging in novelty forms over the years.

▼ Piano problems

A remarkable percentage of the 19thC population was musically literate, and the 1880s saw Germany exporting huge numbers of upright pianos and no home was complete without one. Noise transmission was a problem, however, and a popular item was the glass piano "insulator" for piano feet, made in sets of four, to cut down vibration. Mostly found in clear, amber, and blue, they are simple in form, and made of thick, solid glass. The "mammoth" or "yeti" foot below is appropriately hairy.

A frosted-glass, hairy, "mammoth" piano insulator, 1880s; set of four **$320–400**, each **$64–72**

▼ If the shoe fits

Nostalgia for the 18thC continually manifested itself in sentimental products for mass consumption in the form of novels, films, prints, figurines, and Rococo items ad nauseam. The pressed-glass industry obligingly supplied, and still supplies in the U.S.A., novelty shoes and boots. Most are buckled, and in antiquated styles. These items are closely linked to the glass slipper of Cinderella. A sizeable collection of glass footwear could be assembled, but it would take some time. Intended for displaying flowers, most were probably used to hold spent matches. Sowerby mostly made the design below in clear glass. This 1880s, blue malachite, slag version is attractive and very desirable.

A Sowerby, turquoise-and-white, malachite, slag, buckled shoe, 1880s, **$400–480**

▼ A stiff neck

The large, brown-glass object below was marketed for use as a neck rest. It does not look comfortable, but this was not important as these rests were made to support the necks of the deceased in coffins. They were practical and hygienic, and were removed just before the coffins were closed. Some may have been interred, and future archeologists will no doubt wonder about the significance of these items. Plain, decoratively barren, offbeat items such as this often have amusing explanations attached to them, of great ingenuity and total inaccuracy.

A late 19th–early 20thC neck rest, in amber-coloured glass, **$80–96**

A 1930s, patent safety-razor blade-sharpener, **$32–48**

▲ A close shave

In 1904, King Camp Gillette finally patented his safety razor, invented in 1895. As the blades blunted prematurely, various gadgets appeared over the years that were guaranteed to resharpen and extend the life of each blade. Of more practical use was this 1930s sharpener, on which a flexible blade glided up and down the slope. Such items can be found in the original packaging, with instruction leaflet.

A large, uranium "vaseline" glass, opalescent pike flower-trough, c.1890, **$400–480**

A Sowerby, novelty bucket, in tortoiseshell glass, c.1882, **$240–320**

A small, opalescent, shallow basket, net design, 1880s, **$80–128**

▲ Plagiarism?

It is not unusual to find different-sized versions of the same basic form, and this is the case with regard to the pike shown above, which is the larger version of the one shown on p.36. Molineaux, Webb & Co., Manchester, made both of these from 1885. Sometimes, however, it can be confusing to find a version of something you already have, but without marks, and with subtle differences. Plagiarism was common, and a great deal of contemporary copying went on. In North America the problem of reproductions is a major one; it has, so far, not affected British popular glass.

▲ Novelty colors

The 1882 Sowerby catalog is a treasure-trove of knick-knacks. The tiny bucket above, no. 1566, commands about four times the price of the same item in plain, clear colours. Tortoiseshell glass was not often used, and it is the glass color that affects price here more than the shape. It is the pecking order of scarcity that matters, and this has been established by dealers and collectors over the years. No records exist of how many items were made in the various colors, so rarity is established by what turns up.

▲ Endless novelty

There was, undoubtedly, a limit to the interest that could be sustained in the pattern-making departments of the popular-glass factories. There were hundreds of items that verged on the dull, and this stultification still applies. The shallow basket shown above bears a design that resembles twisted chicken wire, Japanese net designs, or Venetian open-work twisted-glass baskets; it depends on your point of view. Dating from the 1880s, it was probably intended to look Japanese. Items such as this are interesting rather than exciting, run of the mill rather than leading edge. There is a general price bracket for such items, indicated above.

A selection of tiny, cocktail ashtrays, Czech, 1930s, **$56–112** each

▲ **Cocktail customs**
Accessories needed for a successful cocktail party in the 1930s included discreet, but strategically placed, tiny trays on which cigarettes could be stubbed out and discarded. These protected furniture without creating the distasteful middens of smoldering stubs that a large ashtray invariably encourages. The splendid mold-cutters of Bohemia, where there was a long-standing training program based on gem- and medal-cutting, were able to produce exquisitely detailed trays such as those shown above. The itaglio designs, of great variety, in the bases are sand-blasted to give an attractive modeled effect.

A small, slag-glass buckled hat, c.1890, **$120–160**

▲ **Hat tricks**
Glass hats were made in many shapes and sizes, and all are keenly collected by more than one group of collectors. Larger hats can cost up to five time the price of more modest examples. Stylistically they recall the late 18th and early 19thC. These hats go well with the many shoes similar to the one shown on p.53. As well as being collected by pressed-glass enthusiasts, hats are also generally collected in all forms, including free-formed examples, together with glass walking-sticks. Prices reflect this demand.

A 1930s, flower-bowl girl, in frosted green glass, **$48–64**

◀ **1930s flower bowls include pierced "frogs"**
"Flower bowl" is the generic, not the literal, name for a pierced form in which flowers could be arranged. Some "frogs" are figural – Peter Pan, and muslin-swirled ladies, were fashionable. A separate ornament, such as "Windy Wendy", shown here, could be placed in a shallow bowl to appear to be surrounded by a floating flower meadow. The shallow float bowls were filled with flower heads to create miniature table-top ponds, reflecting the taste for table toys and decorations.

Fakes & reproductions

Many items of popular glass have been reproduced, including near replicas that were made shortly after the commercial success of the original. The market is led by collectors, particularly in the U.S.A., and this has produced a confused modern output aimed at collectors, to fill gaps caused by inadequate supplies of the original, as well as supplying attractive, completely new items. Old molds are quite sturdy, and are now valuable in their own right. Some new molds are cut from old designs, some new items are from molds cut in retrospective style. Before buying, ask the dealer if an item is old, and obtain a properly formulated, descriptive invoice. This can come in handy if the item is subsequently found not to be that for which it was invoiced.

A modern, amber-glass reproduction of an early, pressed-glass, dolphin candlestick, 1960s, **$80–96**

▼ Old ideas in new glass

The amber candlestick shown left is a good example of a modern reproduction being a synthesis of earlier, and highly desirable, pressed-glass types. Dolphin candlesticks are prime specimens of 19thC style, and the warmth of amber glass epitomizes the cosy glow and heat of candlelight. Many firms produced such sticks originally, and it is difficult to say precisely, except with marked examples, which modern factories were responsible for the new ones. With dolphin candlesticks, and there are many, ask the dealer if you are unsure of the age of the item, and relate his answer to the price in an unhurried, considered examination.

▶ Figural fakes

Attractive color, in this case a turquoise that recalls the splendid Sèvres bleu céleste, allied to an eye-catching form, can override the cautious sensibilities of even the most experienced collector. This pigmy squirrel on a giant acorn, together with a robin on a stemmed, twiggy nest, is modern, as are large and attractive covered urns of the same color. Other figural fakes exist, and great caution is needed. Most resemble French Vallerysthal models. The glass is often badly finished, with evidence of leaking, ageing molds.

A reproduction squirrel & acorn covered dish, in opaque turquoise glass, 1980s, **$64–80**

▼ Burma, USA

"Burmese" glass was a most attractive 19thC U.S. innovation, later used by Webbs, containing uranium for warm yellow, and heat-reactive gold for shaded, rose-pink effects. It was a success, particularly for Fairy-Light shades, transmitting a warm, flattering, soft light. The Fenton Art Glass Company has successfully reproduced a great deal of this Burmese glass, most of which is marked on the mold. This small "votive" light is not marked. It could be mistaken for a 19thC example, but they mostly resemble the forms shown on p.30.

An unmarked, Burmese, "votive" light, Fenton, 1980s, **$48–64**

▼ Cute and adorable

Much modern "old" pressed glass is designed to be cute, and to appeal to those collectors who cannot resist the adorable. Anything depicting cats walks off the shelves. This Westmoreland, U.S.A., novelty bears its original label, which is often relocated to the base, but is seen here in its original point-of-sale location. This attractive item is finished in acid-treated lime-yellow, but is known in other colors and finishes. Not originally exported, such items wend their way to Europe via collectors, who are inadvertently causing confusion as these pieces circulate in unusual numbers round the markets.

A Westmoreland, puss-in-boot novelty, c.1980s, **$56–72**

A Czech car mascot, borrowed from Lalique, 1930s, **$800–960**

New for old

Reproduction glass that is marked is easily identified as being new. However, modern glass pressed in old molds tends to use only novelty forms, and attractive ideas in alluring colors in order to sell. Sold originally as "new" antiques, these unmarked items are being accepted as old as they travel the markets. It is all collectible, but prices must be for "new" and not for "old."

▼ Imitation or reproduction?

The prestige of Lalique, and the look of his molded glass launched wholesale plagiarism of his ideas. It was easy to produce similarly manufactured "copies." None were marked "Lalique" at the time, but some have been "enhanced." This mascot is based on Longchamps of Lalique. It lacks the convincing artistry of the original moldwork, but is still rare and attractive. All car mascots are much sought after.

PODR & trademarks

Most popular glass is unmarked. Examples that are marked are more keenly sought after, and often cost more simply because of the mark. Unfortunately the mark is incorrectly interpreted, and attracts more attention than the quality of the piece. The mark is simply there as a trademark, and should not be used as an indicator of quality.

The remarkable *Glasmarken Lexikon, 1600–1945, Europa and Nordamerika* by Carolus Hartmann, Arnoldsche, Stuttgart, Germany, 1977, will resolve most marks on all types of glass. It is also available on CD-ROM.

(Anchor) Hocking Glass Company, Lancaster, Ohio, 1905–1937

Anchor-Hocking Glass, U.S.A., from 1937

Cambridge Glass Co., Cambridge, Ohio, 1901–58. Some molds sold to Imperial

Near-Cut Found on some Cambridge Glass items with imitative, cut-glass patterns

NEAR-CUT

George Davidson, (Davidson's), Gateshead, Tyne and Wear, U.K.

John Derbyshire, Manchester, U.K.

Federal Glass, Columbus, Ohio. This mark is often said to be "Fenton", which it is not

Fenton Art Glass Company, Williamstown, West Virginia. Only used on glass made from the 1960s. Not found on old Fenton glass, which is unmarked

Henry Greener, Sunderland, Tyne and Wear, U.K., first mark used 1875–85

Henry Greener, second mark used 1885–1900

Hazel-Atlas Glass Company, Washington, Pennsylvania, and other sites in Ohio and West Virginia

Heisey Glass Company,
U.S.A.

Imperial Glass, Bellaire, Ohio;
early "Iron Cross" mark

Mark of **Imperial Glass**
on special pressed items,
shades, vases, and plates,
mostly of the 1920s

Mark of **Imperial Glass,**
from c.1910, on pressed,
imitative, cut-glass patterns

IG mark of Imperial Glass
from 1960s

LIG mark of Imperial Glass
when operated by Lenox Inc.
from 1972

ALIG mark of Imperial Glass
when operated by Arthur
Lorch, 1981–82

NI mark of "New Imperial"
glass when operated by
Robert Stahl, 1982–84

Jeanette Glass Company,
Jeanette, Pennsylvania

McKee Glass Company,
Jeanette, Pennsylvania.
Operated by Jeanette Glass
Company from 1961

Northwood Glass Company,
Wheeling, West Virginia.
Sometimes found without
circle, or, rarely, with
a double circle

**Sowerby's Ellison
Glassworks.** Gateshead,
Tyne and Wear, U.K.

**Patent Office Design
Registration Marks** (PODR
marks) used in the 19thC
as a deterrent to copyists

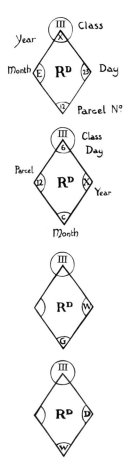

Where to buy & see

Popular molded glassware is sold generally, and is rarely featured in major auction-house sales. Collectors need to attend fairs regularly, and should build up a circuit of local stores and dealers in order to establish relationships that will ensure first refusal of choice items. The huge U.K. Newark and Ardingly fairs are good places to go, but there tends to be too much dealer picking before the punters arrive. The big antiques malls in the U.S.A. overflow with pressed glass, but much is new or reproduction. and great caution is needed. Travelers should consult guidebooks for details of flea markets and fairs in Europe: Berlin, Bratislava, Budapest, Charleroi, Lille, Paris, Prague, Warsaw, and Vienna, are happy hunting grounds. The Internet is now a major market site for finding glass for sale, and sites should be explored, albeit with caution as to condition. Pressed glass can be seen at the following places, but check for details of current displays, temporary exhibitions, and closures.

The Glass Gallery
Victoria & Albert Museum
London, U.K.

Broadfield House Glass Museum
Kingswinford, West Midlands, U.K.

Manchester City Art Gallery and Museum
Manchester, U.K.

Shipley Art Gallery
Gateshead, Tyne and Wear, U.K.

Sunderland Museum and Art Gallery
Sunderland, Tyne and Wear, U.K.

Corning Museum of Glass
Corning, New York

The Metropolitan Museum of Art
New York

Oglebay Institute Glass Museum
Wheeling

Sandwich Glass Museum
Sandwich

Finnish Glass Museum
Riihimäki, Finland

Glass Museum
Växjo, Sweden

Pilkington Museum of Glass
St. Helens, Lancashire, U.K.

Wheaton Village Museum of American Glass
New Jersey

Toledo Museum of Glass
Toledo, Ohio

Fenton Museum
Williamstown, Virginia

Glass Museum
Jablonec, Czech Republic

Applied Arts Museum
Prague, Czech Republic

Musée des Arts Decoratifs
Paris, France

The Carnival Glass Society (UK)
PO Box 14, Hayes
Middlesex, UB3 5NU, U.K.

What to read

The Internet is the best place to find and buy specialist books – both Amazon and Book-Find offer an excellent service; many associated booksellers offer a "wants" service.

Baker, Gary E., Eige, G. Eason et. al. *Wheeling Glass 1829–1939* (Oglebay Institute Glass Museum, U.S.A., 1994)

Baker, John & Crowe, Kate *A Collector's Guide to Jobling 1930s Decorative Glass* (Tyne and Wear Museums, U.K., 1985)

Belknap, E.M. *Milk Glass* (Crown Publishers, U.S.A., 1974)

Burns, Carl O. *The Collector's Guide to Northwood's Carnival Glass* (L-W Book Sales, U.S.A., 1994)

Cottle, Simon *Sowerby Gateshead Glass* (Tyne and Wear Museums Service, U.K., 1986)

Dodsworth, Roger 'The Manchester Glass Industry' (*The Glass Circle*, Vol. 4, 1982, pp64–83)

Doty, David *A Field Guide to Carnival Glass* (The Glass Press, U.S.A., 1998)

Florence, Gene *Depression Glass* (Collector Books, U.S.A., 1976, many editions to date); *Elegant Glassware of the Depression Era* (Collector Books, U.S.A., 1983); *Kitchen Glassware of the Depression Years* (Collector Books, U.S.A., 1983); and **Hajdamach, Charles R.** *British Glass 1800–1914* (Antique Collectors' Club, Woodbridge, Suffolk, U.K., 1991)

Heacock, William *Custard Glass, from A to Z* (Antique Publications, U.S.A., 1976); *Fenton Glass, the Second Twenty-Five Years, 1931–1955* (O-Val Advertising Corp., U.S.A., 1980); *Opalescent Glass from A to Z* (Antique Publications, U.S.A., 1975).

Measell, James & Wiggins, Berry *Harry Northwood: The Wheeling Years 1901–25* (Antique Publications, U.S.A., 1991)

Husfloen, Kyle *Collector's Guide to American Pressed Glass 1825–1915* (Wallace-Homestead Book Company, U.S.A., 1992)

Lattimore, Colin, R. *English 19th-Century Press-Moulded Glass* (Barrie & Jenkins, London, U.K., 1979)

Lee, Ruth Webb *Antique Fakes & Reproductions* (author, U.S.A., 1938; enlarged and revised edition, 1950)

Rose, James H. *American Glass Cup Plates* (Charles E. Tuttle Company, U.S.A., 1984; first published 1948)

Luckey, Carl F. *An Identification & Value Guide to Depression Era Glassware* (Books Americana, U.S.A., 1983)

Morris, Barbara *Victorian Table Glass and Ornaments* (Barrie & Jenkins, London, U.K.,1978)

Murray, Shelagh *The Peacock and the Lions: The Story of Pressed Glass of the North East of England* (Oriel Press, Stocksfield, U.K., 1982)

Nelson, Kirk, J. *50 Favorites: Early American Pressed Glass Goblets* (University of Wisconsin-Stevens Point, U.S.A., 1993)

Notley, Raymond *Carnival Glass* (Shire Publications, Princes Risborough, U.K., 5th Edition, 1997); *Pressed Flint Glass* (Shire Publications, Princes Risborough, U.K., 1986)

Slack, Raymond *English Pressed Glass, 1830-1900* (Barrie & Jenkins, London, U.K., 1987)

Spillman, Jane Shadel *American and European Pressed Glass in the Corning Museum of Glass* (The Corning Museum of Glass, U.S.A., 1981)

Thistlewood, Glen & Stephen *Carnival Glass: The Magic and the Mystery* (Schiffer Publishing Ltd., U.S.A., 1998)

Thompson, Jenny *The Identification of English Pressed Glass, 1842–1908* (author, 1989); *A Supplement to the Identification of English Pressed Glass, 1842–1908* (author, 1993)

Walker, John & Elizabeth *Pressed Glass in America: Encyclopedia of the First Hundred Years, 1825–1925* (Antique Acres Press, 1985)

Glossary

arsenical oxide was used into the 19thC as a decolorant powder in the batch, to clear sand of its natural-iron greenish tinge

batch the basic mixture of sand and soda, that is melted overnight in fireclay pots to produce molten glass ready for production

black basaltes a Wedgwood stoneware color, which was replicated by Manchester glassworks

blow-molding a bubble of molten glass is expanded inside a closed wood or iron mold, which opens to release a hollow object

Bristol blue a generic description for the color of blue glass that has been made using cobalt oxide

Burmese glass an opaque, heat-sensitive glass

Carnival Glass a pressed or blow-molded glass that is sprayed with metallic salts when hot, to produce a shimmering iridescent effect

cobalt the oxide used to produce a rich blue in glass

custard glass a creamy-colored, uranium glass, made opaque with white oxides

Depression Glass American, 1930s and 1940s, mechanically molded suites of table glass, made with machine-friendly shallow patterns

flint glass another name for clear glass

gold ruby glass another way of describing old red glass

iridescence a thin layer of metallic salts applied to glass to produce lusters

malachite an opaque pressed glass which is marbled together

marigold a name to describe golden iridescence on clear glass

milk glass a flint glass made opaque by the use of tin oxide

mold, metal expensive, permanent, finely-cut, and chased metal forms of iron

mold, wood short-lived, cheap, hinged, wooden molds used for limited production of blow-molded hollow items

opalescent glass a glass that betrays a fiery heart when held to the light

peach opal(escent) a name to describe golden iridescence applied to clear opalescent glass

Pearline a name used by Davidson for its blue or "Primrose" opalescent glass

pressed glass soft, molten glass is forced into patterned, closed, iron molds, which open to release the finished, patterned form of variable thickness

Primrose the name of Davidson's yellow opalescent glass

Queen's Ware a name borrowed from Wedgwood by Sowerby for an opaque, warm cream, vitro-porcelain glass, which imitated late 18thC creamware

red glass (old) contains copper and gold, and needs high temperature re-heating to develop the color

red glass (new) made from the mid-1920s, contains copper and selenium, and is suitable for pressed glass as a lower re-heating temperature is needed to develop the color

sand/silica the basic ingredient of glass melts at a very high temperature, and needs fluxes, such as soda, to melt at a more viable and practical temperature

slag a marbled, opaque, pressed glassware, which briefly incorporated metal industry by-products

soda the flux used, with others such as lime, to lower the temperature at which sand (silica) melts

uranium glass an acid-green or yellow radio-active glass that contains uranium oxide

uranium oxide a powder, added to the batch to produce sharp yellows or greens

vaseline glass an anachronistic name for acid-colored green or yellow glass

vitro-porcelain a glass that looks like ceramic

zoomorphic an object in the form of an animal, or part of an animal

Index

Acknowledgments
Octopus Publishing Group Ltd/A. J. Photographics/Broadfield House Glass Museum 7, 11cl, 14l, 16t, 17t, 17b, 18b, 22r, 26l, 26r, 27c, 28b, 30l, 31b, 34l, 42b, 46b, 48t, 48b, 49t, 49b, 50r, 51t, 52t, 52b, 53t, 53c, 53b, 54tl; **/A. J. Photographics/Raymond Notley** 1, 5, 6, 8tl, 8br, 9tl, 9tcr, 9bl, 10c, 10bc, 11cb, 12tl, 12tr, 12ct, 13tc, 13cr, 14r, 15c, 15b, 16b, 17c, 19bl, 21t, 21c, 21b, 23t, 23c, 23b, 24t, 24b, 25l, 25rt, 25c, 28t, 29t, 29bl, 31t, 31c, 32b, 33t, 33bl, 36t, 36b, 37t, 37br, 38l, 38r, 39t, 39c, 39b, 40l, 40r, 40c, 41l, 41r, 41c, 42t, 43tl, 43tr, 43b, 44l, 44r, 45t, 45c, 46t, 49c, 50l, 54tr, 55t, 56l, 56r, 57l; **/Steve Tanner/D. & P. Atkinson** 15t, 18t, 19t, 19br, 20l, 20r, 22l, 27t, 27b, 29br, 30r, 32t, 33bl, 34r, 35t, 35c, 35b, 37bl, 45b, 47l, 47r, 51bl, 54b, 55c, 55b, 57r, 57c; **/Steve Tanner/Gillian Neale 2;** **/Steve Tanner/Private Collection** 47c, 51br

The author would like to thank, most sincerely, Mika Öljymäki and Liz Stubbs, all the staff of Broadfield House Glass Museum, and, most especially, Phyllis and Don Atkinson, for their individual help, invaluable expert advice, and permanent encouragement.